*Presented to
the Santa Cruz
Public Libraries by*

A GENEROUS DONOR

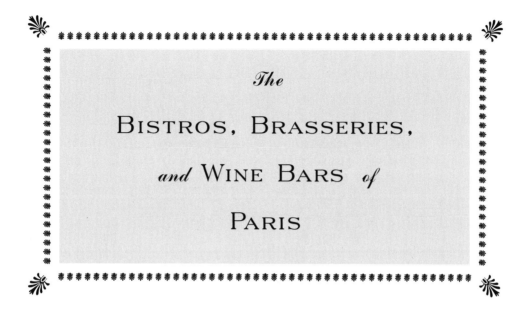

The

BISTROS, BRASSERIES,

and WINE BARS *of*

PARIS

Other books by Daniel Young

Made in Marseille
The Rough Guide to New York City Restaurants
The Paris Café Cookbook

The

BISTROS, BRASSERIES,

and WINE BARS

of PARIS

EVERYDAY RECIPES
FROM THE REAL PARIS

DANIEL YOUNG

PHOTOGRAPHS BY DANIEL YOUNG

WILLIAM MORROW
An Imprint of HarperCollinsPublishers

HarperCollins books may be purchased for educational, business, or sales promotional use. For information please write: Special Markets Department, HarperCollins Publishers, 10 East 53rd Street, New York, NY 10022.

FIRST EDITION

Designed by Leah Carlson-Stanisic

Printed on acid-free paper

Library of Congress Cataloging-in-Publication Data

Young, Daniel.
  The bistros, brasseries, and wine bars of Paris : everyday recipes from the real Paris / Daniel Young.—1st ed.
      p.   cm.
  Includes index.
  ISBN-13: 978-0-06-059073-4
  ISBN-10: 0-06-059073-4
  1. Cookery, French.   2. Bars (Drinking establishments).   I. Title.

TX719.Y64   2006
641.5944—dc22
                                                                    2005049139

06   07   08   09   10   ❖/RRD   10   9   8   7   6   5   4   3   2   1

FOR VIVIAN

Contents

....

Acknowledgments

....

THE HOSPITALITY AND CONVIVIALITY SO PARTICULAR TO PARISIAN BISTROS, BRASSERIES, and wine bars, as opposed to mere restaurants, were put to a severe test during the writing of this cookbook. I depended upon the cooperation, affability, and know-how of the chefs, owners, servers, and habitués at the establishments portrayed here in recipes, words, and photos. Often I am asked, "How do you get the chefs to give you their best recipes?" It certainly helps that I become a familiar face in their dining rooms before I introduce myself and reveal my intentions. Their appetite for publicity is another factor. But ultimately it is a matter of my convincing them to share very good food with a receptive, discerning, and extremely grateful audience, a logical extension both of their daily work and lifelong passion.

I owe a debt of gratitude to Sophie Morel and Michèle Villemur for granting me complete, behind-the-scenes access to the Flo brasseries and to Alain Ducasse and his press attaché, Hélène Barbier, for their enthusiastic support. I also wish to thank my friends and dining companions Alain Boulet, Jeanne Boulet, David Brower, Steven Forbis, Matthieu Galian, Gael Greene, Dorie Greenspan, Gérard Hausman, Juliette Joste, Agnès Lozet, Steven Richter, Hélène Samuel, and Alain Weill for helping me sample and critique the dishes up for consideration, either out at the bistros, brasseries, and wine bars or at recipe-testing sessions in my Paris apartment.

I also benefited from the backing of my steadfast pals Mary Barone, Diana Biederman, Steven Biondolillo, Nina Blaine, Mitchell Brower, Ray Chen, Alan Cohen, Anne de Ravel,

Mark Giles, Robert Lovenheim, JoAnn Makovitzky, Neil Manson, Anahita Mekanik, Marco Moreira, Simon Oren, Arthur Schwartz, Jeff Weinstein, Olivier Wittman, and Pamela Wittman. I enjoyed the love and support of my parents Mimi Young and David Young; my brothers Bill Young and Roy Young; my sisters-in law Sharon Baumgold and Laurie Young; my nieces Elizabeth, Hava, Molly, and Shoshana; my nephew Aaron; and my cousins Marilyn Goodman and Stacey Facter.

1001 *mercis* to my agent, Alice Martell, for her abundant intelligence, class, and loyalty. I feel most fortunate to have worked again with the cookbook pros at Morrow, most notably editor Harriet Bell, her assistant Lucy Baker, designer Leah Carlson-Stanisic, and, in our third rewarding collaboration, copy and production editor Ann Cahn, and publicist Carrie Weinberg. A very special thank you to Susan Friedland for commissioning this title.

In the course of writing this book, I met and married my wonderful co-conspirator, Vivian Constantinopoulos. Dining out repeatedly with the love of my life did not, however, bring me any closer to determining what is the most romantic seating position at a Parisian bistro, brasserie, or wine bar: face-to-face, side-by-side, or at a right angle. Far from feeling frustrated I look forward to exploring these configurations further with Vivian for decades of dinners to come.

❀

Quelle Est la Différence?

What, you ask, is the difference between a bistro, a brasserie, and a wine bar? Good question: During the past two years I've consulted dozens of Parisian restaurateurs, chefs, waiters, bartenders, diners, etymologists, lexicographers, journalists, cultural historians, and hairdressers on this very matter.

The responses, varying considerably in perspective, tone, and length but rarely in their utter certainty, have been a continuous source of surprise and enlightenment, as much now as at the onset. And so it is only a minor disappointment that I've yet to hear any Parisian, not even the pillars of these establishments, the ever-present habitués who appear to physically hold up their wood, Formica, or zinc-style bar tops, adequately explain the distinctions among these familiar haunts.

The flawed definitions and blurred comparisons reflect the evolution not only of these three treasured institutions but also of what is expected of them. Parisians are ambivalent toward change and accept, embrace, or reject it at their own pace and rarely without the familiar lament *ce n'est pas comme avant*—"it's not like it used to be." But though they crave the old-fashioned virtues of the classic bistro, brasserie, and wine bar, few truly want these establishments to operate exactly as they did before. It's illustrative to recall that all three institutions began with an emphasis on liquid over solid refreshment. Cooking was almost an after-thought. Many Parisians over fifty still don't regard bistros as places to seek out a meal.

"At a bistro you only drink," says Bernard Marmels, a veteran *directeur* (floor manager) at the brasserie Au Pied de Cochon, explaining the difference between a bistro and brasserie.

That dated view notwithstanding, today's bistros operate first and foremost as dining places, a growing number of them exceptional ones. The chefs at the finest modern, neo, or gastro bistros can garner the same acclaim and reservations backlog as their counterparts at highly rated, Michelin-starred restaurants, many of whom are expanding into the bistro trade themselves. And the traditional wine bar with only cheeses and charcuterie to feed its clientele is vanishing from the scene. The bar needs a kitchen, too.

"Habits have changed," notes François Briclot of Le Rouge-Gorge, a wine bar with a bistro-style menu. "If you only give them *saucisson* you're finished."

The understanding of these terms is also complicated by their current vogue. The instant cachet attached to a new place calling itself a bistro, a brasserie, or a *bar à vin*, as opposed to a mere restaurant, encourages opportunistic entrepreneurs in France and elsewhere to apply these buzzwords to establishments that resemble their forebears in name or decor only. And because the genuine articles are colloquial locales revered as much for their discomforts as their comforts, posting one of three B-words outside a new restaurant can turn limitations into advantages. A bistro, for example, makes tiny tables, rickety chairs, zero elbow room, mismatching stainless-steel cutlery, and waiters who editorialize on your food selections appear trendy. Only at a brasserie can clamor, brusque table service, precooked main courses, and unrelenting *rapidité* be linked, and rightly so, with high style and glamour. Having a glass of wine poured from a previously opened bottle is a privilege, not a sacrilege, at a wine bar.

But perhaps the biggest obstacle to nailing down the differences among bistro, brasserie, and wine bar is their shared identity. Together they nourish and sustain the Paris of Parisians—the real and everyday Paris—with local food, flavor, style, sophistication, personality, and attitude. Like English pubs, Greek tavernas, Italian trattorias, and American diners, they are places where people go out to feel at home, only it isn't just any home we're talking about. If a routine Tuesday night dinner in Paris is superior in fundamental ways to a celebratory Saturday soiree nearly anywhere else, it is a happy consequence of the extraordinary extent to which its best bistros, brasseries, and wine bars exalt the ordinary, from *vins ordinaires*, *plats du jour*, and rustic fruit tarts to ritual gestures, familiar faces, and replayed dialogue. Indeed, recognition itself is as much the ultimate reward for Henri Gonzales, a *maître d'hôtel* (headwaiter) who eagerly cultivates regulars—his regulars—at the brasserie La Coupole as it is for the woman of a certain age who comes in alone for lunch every Sunday, sits at the same table in his section, orders the same fish dish, and, after her first taste, beckons Gonzales over to deliver the same critique and elicit the same response:

"*Monsieur!*"
"*Oui, Madame.*"
"The sole, it's not like it was before."
"Before what, *Madame?*"

The alternate and most common French spelling of bistro has a silent *t* on the end. Yet finding the term *bistrot* stenciled on a plate-glass window, while helpful in this guessing game, is no guarantee the premises within fit that particular "B" classification to a T. The same is true of places that emboss their menu covers with the term *brasserie* or paint *bar à vin* across the awnings.

The Brasserie de la Poste is more bistro than brasserie, a conclusion its proprietor, Jérôme Blanchard, not only shares but encourages.

Le Baratin, though certainly the wine bar it purports to be, is a purer example of the classic Parisian bistro than scores of small restaurants dressed and named for the part. Le Chantefable is without question a bistro, or so says its owner, Pierre Ayral, but it also meets the central criteria of a brasserie and a wine bar. So which one is it? And what exactly are the criteria useful in making that determination?

Here then is a twenty-question checklist, which, though neither scientific nor infallible, will help delineate the differences. If the place under consideration has no *plats du jour*, no bar to speak of, no overcrowded tables, and no Parisian soul, chances are it's only a restaurant.

The calm before lunch service at Le Bistrot Paul Bert.

	BISTRO	BRASSERIE	WINE BAR
1) Does it serve more than five different wines by the glass?	Sometimes	Sometimes	Usually
2) Does it serve tapas-sized plates?	Rarely	Rarely	Usually
3) Does it sell bottles of wine to carry out?	Rarely	Rarely	Usually
4) Does it have continuous food service throughout the day?	Rarely	Usually	Usually
5) Does it serve draft beer?	Rarely	Usually	Usually
6) Does it serve oysters on the half shell?	Sometimes	Usually	Rarely
7) Does it serve choucroute?	Rarely	Usually	Rarely
8) Is the entire menu hand-printed in chalk on a slate board?	Usually	Rarely	Usually
9) Does it have fine table linens at mealtimes?	Sometimes	Usually	Rarely
10) Is service intended to be extremely fast?	Sometimes	Usually	Sometimes
11) Does it have a small, zinc-style bar?	Sometimes	Rarely	Usually
12) Are there fewer than twenty-five tables?	Usually	Rarely	Usually
13) Are the tables closely spaced?	Usually	Usually	Usually
14) Does the menu change drastically from season to season?	Usually	Rarely	Sometimes
15) Does it offer a *plat du jour*?	Usually	Usually	Sometimes
16) Is the service staff dressed in black and white uniforms?	Rarely	Usually	Rarely
17) Do the waiters carry trays?	Rarely	Usually	Rarely
18) Are there lots of mirrors hung on the walls?	Sometimes	Usually	Sometimes
19) Is the word *"chez"* in the name of the business?	Sometimes	Rarely	Rarely
20) Does it have a terrace?	Usually	Sometimes	Rarely

Y = USUALLY   **Y** = SOMETIMES   **Y** = RARELY

THE BISTRO

Parisians inside as well as outside the restaurant trade take great pleasure in recounting the origins of the term *bistro(t)*. They date its infiltration into the French language to sometime after the Russian occupation of Paris in 1814. Hungry Cossacks demanding prompt attention at local pubs would shout out *"Bistro,"* a Russian word for *quick*. More than just a good yarn, it is a testament to the hospitable and possibly also the forgiving nature of Parisians that they attrib-

ute the naming of so vital a part of their patrimony to foreigners, members of an occupying army no less, without the support of logic, factual evidence, or the Académie Française, the official French authority on the usage and vocabulary of the French language.

The Académie Française dates the first attestation of the word *bistro* to 1884—much too late to lend credence to the tale. Two alternative hypotheses are judged to be plausible: (1) That it comes from the identically pronounced *bistraud*, the helper of a wine merchant and

Aux Lyonnais, an 1890 Parisian bouchon *restored by the great chef Alain Ducasse.*

(2) That it comes from *bist(r)oille,* a dark-colored or twice-mixed beverage. In these cases the establishment would have taken its name either from the clerk's occupation, as in the phrase *aller chez le bistraud,* "going to the wine seller's place," or his house wine. Regardless, it is not terribly difficult to fathom why the raconteurs' fidelity to the officially discredited version persists. The story is a lot more entertaining.

Bistro-type establishments existed long before anyone decided to call them bistros. In the early nineteenth century the French city of Lyon already had its *bouchon,* a homegrown variation of the pit-stop pub whose unfussy manners and rustic regional fare were models for the Parisian bistro. Le Procope, believed to be the first Parisian cafe, opened in 1686. Taverns within the hexagon that now constitutes France date back at least as far as the first century B.C., when Julius Caesar alluded to them in *The Gallic Wars.*

THE AUVERGNATS

The story of the modern Parisian bistro essentially starts with the laborers who migrated to the French capital from the rural area of Auvergne in south-central France during the mid and late nineteenth century. The so-called Auvergnats typically started out as water carriers, filling and refilling their buckets at public fountains, balancing them over their shoulders, and hauling them up and down the winding stairways of six-story apartment houses. Those who either thrived in this grueling work or were sufficiently desperate to get out of it expanded into the distribution of wood, coal, and wine, much of it produced in Auvergne. Many opened small depots on or near the rue de Lappe, in the vicinity of the Bastille. A glass of red wine was soon served from behind the counter and, later, a homemade *plat du jour*, usually prepared by the owner's wife, to go with it. These primitive mom-and-pop bistros spread throughout Paris to welcome displaced provincials from all over France. Steadfastly loyal to their own, the *bistrotiers* purchased their provisions from fellow Auvergnats. Their counters were often plated in tin shipped north from mills in Auvergne. Parisians and expats mistook the tin for zinc, ignoring all evidence to the contrary, and the wrong metallic element became the enduring symbol of a bistro's conducive warmth and hospitality.

The current and near universal allure of those tin-plated "Zincs" belies the historically humble image of the Parisian bistro. Likewise the homespun tableware, old display advertising, and broken-tile mosaics that add a veneer of vintage authenticity to retro hot spots. The bistros were long shunned by middle and upper-class Parisians as coarse, lowly, working-class joints. The bourgeois favored more elegant cafés like Le Procope, Café de la Paix, and Fouquet's. Bernard Brouillet, owner of the revered bistro Chez Georges, remembers the expression *aller au bistrot*—"going to the bistro"—as being a pejorative one. Maybe that's why so many Auvergnats took to calling their bistros cafés.

Bistros experienced something of a renaissance during the years immediately following the liberation of Paris in 1944 not so much by shedding stereotypes as living up to them. Their working-class sociability, fed by easygoing banter and recurrent comings and goings, satisfied a need shared by Parisians freed from occupation to gather where they would feel most welcome. Their creature comforts restored the collective well-being while recalling a simpler time. Moreover, they were cheap.

PEASANT CHIC

The ongoing bistro revival of the last twenty years draws on an appetite for down-to-earth simplicity as well as a nostalgia for two kinds of ritualistic ribbings: the harmless wisecrack served up daily by the impish host exploiting his habitués' foibles and the elbow poke inadvertently delivered by a demonstrative stranger seated at an abutting table. Habits that used to invite scorn have become fashionable. This turnaround might be compared to changing tastes in French bread. Well-to-do Parisians traditionally preferred white breads while working-class Parisians were compelled to buy cheaper, darker *pains noirs* made with rye, buckwheat, barley, and other whole-grain flours. Lately it is the darker peasant breads that are sought by trendy and affluent Parisians, who must now pay a premium for *pains noirs*. Plain white baguettes have fallen in stature, relative cost, and the care and attention the city's finest bakers afford them.

The bistros in the current vanguard, most of them *pain noir* proponents, generally have a more single-minded approach to food procurement and preparation than their predecessors of sixty, forty, and, with several notable exceptions, thirty years ago. That most now have a professionally trained chef in the kitchen is only a small part of the story. Many home-schooled or self-taught bistro cooks no doubt took their cooking—and had loyal patrons who took their cooking—very seriously. That's still true: Le Baratin's Raquel Carena learned everything she knows from cookbooks, beginning her education with the great French chef Paul Bocuse's *La Cuisine du Marché*. She is among the bistro chefs most highly praised by her most highly praised colleagues. Rather, it is the central role of the chef that is a recent phenomenon. The better bistros now operate primarily as sit-down restaurants. If they have bars, and virtually all still do, few have anyone actually drinking at them. The "Zincs" function to a large extent as service counters.

This transformation applies not only to mod-ern standouts like L'Avant-Goût and L'Épi Dupin but also to great classics as they exist now. Brouillet acknowledges that Chez Georges, though revered as a quintessential Parisian bistro, originated as a restaurant, took over a space long occupied by a restaurant, and probably would have been viewed as a restaurant, as opposed to a bistro, a generation ago.

Is the very notion of a classic bistro then something of a modern myth? Not quite. A bistro is above all about conviviality, and there is very little at Chez Georges to interfere with the enjoyment of good food, good drink, and good company. Odd as it is to be continually praising something for its limitations, a full appreciation

of what Parisian bistros have to offer requires a complete understanding of what amenities they swear off. Furnishing one with fine linens, silverware, or crystal would hardly be ruinous. I don't foresee any food critic panning an otherwise outstanding address for having the temerity to replace its stainless-steel cutlery with silver plate. But the addition of anything smacking of luxury would violate an unspoken bargain—and a good bargain it is—between bistro owner and patron that the former not give so much as the appearance of charging the latter for frills and froufrou.

That informal agreement keeps bistros accessible not only to price-sensitive diners but also to young, talented, ambitious, underfinanced chefs who want to go into business on their own. It lets them put their money where our mouths are. Chez Michel, L'Ami Jean, Le Repaire de Cartouche, and Le Beurre Noisette are extraordinary places to visit because their respective chef/proprietors, Thierry Breton, Stéphane Jégo, Rodolphe Paquin, and Thierry Blanqui, are free to pour their resources and energies into the achievement of a single overriding goal: *mettre en valeur*—"showing to best advantage"—the finest and freshest meats, seafood, and seasonal produce available to them at market. That requires them to treat the main ingredients of each dish simply and reverentially, to, in Paquin's words, "concentrate on the cooking rather than forced ideas." Ideally, the original touches these skilled chefs apply to bistro classics neither mask nor alter their essen-

tial character. Overdressing is in every sense a bistro taboo.

The omissions, the foods the bistro chefs don't prepare, are themselves telling. Peruse the menu of just about any upscale, critically acclaimed, gastronomic temple of French cuisine in Paris and, regardless of season, you'll likely find dishes featuring many of the following star ingredients: foie gras, truffles, duck breast, rack of lamb, caviar, lobster, langoustine (spiny lobster or prawn), turbot, sole, cod, *bar de ligne* (line-caught bass). But in France these noble ingredients strain a bistro-sized budget. Seldom do they turn up as title ingredients in the *plats du jour* etched in chalk on slate boards. Though many bistro chefs find it hard to resist foie gras, they employ the other luxury foods sparingly, unless they happen to hear from a colleague or a supplier about a special at Rungis, the complex of wholesale food markets in suburban Paris. "Everything is a question of price," says Jégo, who is forever on the hunt for broken-limbed lobsters selling at a discount. He wastes nothing, extracting every last trace of lobster meat and then using the shells to flavor stocks, sauces, soups, and vinaigrettes.

THE GASTRO BISTRO

Jégo developed his gift for thrift working for more than a decade as the sideman of Yves Camdeborde, the chef who revolutionized Parisian bistro cooking at La Régalade. Camdeborde's mere presence at that remote Left Bank bistro was first viewed as an industry shocker. In 1991 he was playing backup to the great chef Christian Constant and on the path to a Michelin-starred stage of his own when, in his mid-twenties, he moved from the rarefied world of the Hôtel de Crillon and the place de la Concorde to a nondescript bistro on the outer limits of the 14th arrondissement. From that point until his departure in May 2004, Camdeborde mastered a middle ground between refined and rustic, haute cuisine and traditional bistro cooking. He applied a near fanaticism to the selection and preparation of the highest-quality seasonal ingredients. He employed elite ingredients to ennoble humbler meats, poultry, game, and fish. His democratization of fine French cooking placed La Régalade into a new restaurant category: the gastro bistro.

Camdeborde's success and fame inspired other rising-star chefs to quit the employ of larger restaurants and abandon a more secure and traditional career ladder in order to open their own bistros. Several of the chefs featured in this book—Jégo, Paquin, Thierry Faucher—regard Camdeborde as their spiritual father. In a couple of instances he is also their largest investor. Camdeborde's cooking is no longer featured at La Régalade and, as a result, is technically not represented in this book. But if you removed his influence there would be many blank pages.

The bistro's upward climb also got a big push from some giants of the Parisian dining scene. Superstar chefs like Michel Rostang, Guy Savoy,

and Alain Ducasse made it culinarily correct to *aller au bistro* by attaching their names to bistros spun off from their deluxe restaurants. Recipes from two of them, Rostang's Le Bistrot d'à Côté and Ducasse's Aux Lyonnais, are featured in this book. It is nevertheless a bit of a stretch to classify all of these restaurant annexes as genuine bistros, especially when dinner checks approach or surpass $100 per person. Value for money is central to the bistro bargain.

For this book I've applied a rather liberal definition of bistro to encompass modest neighborhood haunts like Clémentine, gastro destinations like L'Entredgeu, and many great meals in between. But I resisted including robotic, soulless, "concept" establishments. Where there's no warmth and no *convivialité*, there's no bistro.

THE BRASSERIE

A brasserie is a waiter in black vest and bow tie, Champagne bucket affixed to silver tray affixed to upward-facing palm, racing down a mosaic-tiled aisle with the urgency of a fireman and the grace of Fred Astaire. A brasserie is a crew of shuckers in sailor suits piling raw oysters on the ice-bedded tiers of a seafood platter stacked as high as a royal wedding cake. A brasserie is a packed terrace on the boulevard Montparnasse, where Joyce, Picasso, Hemingway, Stravinsky, and a colony of artistic geniuses sit on caned chairs, sip drinks, peoplewatch, hobnob, and dream up radically original ways to put off returning to work. A brasserie is you and the love of your life, squeezed into a corner banquette at the intersection of the Belle Époque and the Jazz Age, filling your spoons and each other with the hot chocolate sauce that is slowly melting the vanilla ice cream inserted into crusty pastry puffs in a plate of profiteroles.

Accordingly, there is no stronger evidence of Parisian enchantment, of the City of Light's capacity to extract lustrous pearls from farm-grown oysters than this: A brasserie starts with beer. A brasserie *is* beer.

The word itself comes from *brasseur*, French for "brewer." *Brasserie,* which dates from the year 1268, literally means "brewery." It wasn't until the mid-nineteenth century that it also became synonymous with a tavern. Beer brewed up until that time was too fragile to transport across cities, let alone across continents. Home refrigeration, then nonexistent, did not become common in France until after the Second World War. Beer was mostly consumed inside breweries or the taverns and beer halls attached to them.

The emergence and proliferation of the Parisian brasserie during the second half of the nineteenth century were facilitated by technological and scientific advances and economic conditions. The introduction of the steam engine and commercial refrigeration improved production efficiency. Louis Pasteur solved the problem of beer gone sour, then prevalent in France, by teaching brewers how to cultivate only the right organisms for good beer and kill off bacteria by heating initial sugar solutions to a high temperature. When the epidemics of oid-ium (powdery mildew) and phylloxera (a parasitic insect) decimated vineyards throughout France and doubled the price of wine, Frédéric Bofinger had draft beer with a consistent, unspoiled taste to offer as an affordable alternative at his brasserie on the rue de la Bastille, believed to be the first in Paris.

THE ALSATIAN WHO TOOK THE BASTILLE

Like just about all the pioneers of the Parisian brasserie, Bofinger came to Paris as a refugee from Alsace, a region in northeast France that shares a border with Germany as well as a long heritage of beer brewing and drinking. From the lead-up to the Franco-Prussian War until the annexation of Alsace by Germany in 1871, an estimated fifty thousand people immigrated westward into France. The brasserie Bofinger, opened in 1864, and others of its generation started as minuscule taprooms. To lure more converts from grapes to malt and to compete against the Auvergnat *bistrotiers* clustered on the other side of the Bastille from Bofinger, the brasseries began serving hot food to go with their cold drafts. Typically it was something Alsatian that could be prepared in advance and readied in a flash. *Choucroute garnie*—a copious platter of braised sauerkraut accompanied by a variety of smoked and salted sausages, pork, bacon, potatoes, and juniper berries—was not just a brasserie's *plat du jour*; it was its plate of every day.

The summit of the brasserie's ascension, the main dining room at Bofinger.

The brasseries expanded in number, size, and splendor. From small brewpubs grew beer halls appointed with rich woods, intricate marquetry, and folkloric art in the Alsatian country tradition. Soon wood tabletops were replaced by marble ones. Wood benches were removed for leather banquettes. And French decorative arts from the Second Empire, Art Nouveau, and Art Deco periods transformed these beer-drinking venues into stylized icons of Parisian sophistication. Forget beer. Forget Alsace. These *brasseries du luxe* functioned as grand café-restaurants and, to use the neon vernacular of their heyday, glamorous *bars américains* inspired by a romanticized notion of the American cocktail lounge.

High over Bofinger's main dining room, a glass dome in the ornate Art Nouveau design of glass masters Néret and Royer represents the summit of the brasserie's Parisian ascension. Below, in a landmark grown to house 270 seats and a gazillion bottles of Champagne, the tufted black leather banquettes, looping brass-stemmed wall lamps, tall arched mirrors, exquisite period woodwork, and intermittent whiffs of sauerkraut maintain their power to enthrall. As you push through Bofinger's revolving door there is no host to greet you at the high desk presumably installed to the immediate left for said purpose. A warmhearted *bonjour* awaits you further inside at a reservations podium wedged into a heavily trafficked crossway between the bar, the kitchen, and the approaches to the front, main, and upper-level dining rooms. "The brasserie," explains *directeur* Jean-Luc Blanlot, "must catch the diners' eyes before I do."

THE AUVERGNATS BATTLE BACK

The luminous splendor of Bofinger and other burgeoning brasseries did not escape the notice of the bistro community, especially its representatives hailing from Aveyron, an area on the southwest border of Auvergne that has always been fertile ground for Parisian restaurateurs. Aveyronnais opened two of the most famous Left Bank brasseries, Montparnasse's Le Dôme (today a swank fish restaurant) and La Coupole, and took over a third, the legendary Brasserie Lipp of Saint-Germain-des-Prés. The Alsatian Léonard Lipp sold his ten-table, circa 1880 brasserie to Marcellin Cazes, a onetime water carrier who in 1926 increased Lipp's capacity tenfold to accommodate the who's who of politicians, writers, artists, and actors who would embrace it as their rendezvous. Recognizing the see-and-be-seen imperative of brasserie glamour, the astute Cazes was the first to angle mirrors slightly down from the wall, thus affording those who sat facing in and those passing behind them an unobstructed view of one another.

Few of Cazes's contemporaries sought to rival his house of tilted-down mirrors. Their move onto Alsatian turf grew out of meat-and-potato considerations. The Auvergnats and Aveyronnais viewed the brasserie formula, with its continuous service of rough-and-ready regional cooking, as a natural extension of the bistro. The café-brasseries they installed on busy corners all over town were modest, informal canteens, the Paris equivalents of truck stops, with some subtle differences: Beef bourguignon, cassoulet, and veal blanquette were their blue plate specials; steak tartare, *choucroute garnie*, and *croque monsieur*; their hamburger, hot dogs and sauerkraut, and ham-and-cheese sandwich. That bill of fare, not forgetting omelets, composed salads, and crêpes, was, prior to 1970, the closest thing the city had to fast food. The safe distance between Parisians and the hamburger revolution did not last. Several McDonald's franchises you see at the *portes* of Paris, the main entryways that dot the city's periphery, replaced café-brasseries and influenced others to quicken their food service and cheapen their image.

Brasserie remains an ambiguous designation. The wide disparity between the serviceable canteens and luminous landmarks like Bofinger, Lipp, and La Coupole compels insiders to draw a distinction between the brasserie *du coin* ("local") and the brasserie *du luxe* ("luxurious"). The brasseries whose recipes are featured in this book are all of the *du luxe* variety, though some are more *du luxe* than others. None truly specializes in deluxe cuisine, however polished their black-tie service and glittery seafood platters. They invite trouble for themselves and diners when their French cooking gets fancy.

A more prevalent criticism relates to a formulaic sameness dictated by the restaurant groups that have gobbled up the most famous brasseries. The Groupe Flo, headed by Jean-Paul Bucher, owns, among other brasseries, Bofinger, La Coupole, Balzar, and Julien. Les Frères Blanc have a dozen Parisian brasseries, starting with Au Pied de Cochon, a property which Clément Blanc—the *père* of brothers Jacques and Pierre, the company's founders—purchased some seventy years ago. Descendants of Marcellin Cazes recently sold the Brasserie Lipp to the Groupe Bertrand.

Much is indeed lost when a family-run brasserie is taken over by a restaurant group. Individuality is sacrificed at the expense of organizational efficiency. At the Flo-owned brasseries, for example, central purchasing determines what dinner specials their chefs prepare and their headwaiters push. If it's lobster week at Bofinger, it's lobster week at La Coupole, too. But accusations about their relying on frozen meats and canned vegetables and soups are erroneous, as is the assumption that independent brasseries are immune to rushed, delayed, or sloppily executed meals.

I'm squarely on the side of Parisians who bemoan the homogenizing effect of restaurant group management. To recall the nostalgist's lament, it is not like it was before. But I am quicker to credit Monsieur Bucher of the Groupe Flo in particular for preserving and restoring these landmark brasseries and making them viable businesses in the late twentieth and early twenty-first centuries. And I am grateful to both group and indie brasserie owners for maintaining the clearly defined manners and hierarchy of classic brasserie service. In a restaurant, great service is service you barely notice. In a brasserie, great service is service you can't help but notice. It's a show that's not to be missed.

There are four service ranks in the brasserie: *chef du rang* ("waiter"), *maître d'hôtel* (headwaiter), *directeur adjoint* ("associate floor manager"), and *directeur*.

The *chef du rang*, dressed in black (vest, pants, bow tie, shoes) and white (shirt, apron), is assigned to a station the French call a *rang*—for *row* of tables. He (or, in rare instances, she) must be a swift, smooth, deceptively muscular acrobat able to carry heavy trays from kitchen to dining room and back, dozens of times, without any sign of strain. He is to confine all his sweating, if he must do any of it at all, to the area behind the kitchen door. He also processes orders and checks, sets and clears tables, and, in his spare time, takes dessert requests.

The *maître d'hôtel*, suited in black dinner jacket and bow tie, performs few tasks that put the perfect crease in his slacks at risk. Rarely does he depart from his *rang* of up to a dozen tables. He greets diners, takes orders, and watches over both. A master of inflection, he is able to utter *"oui, madame"* as a declaration of love one moment and an expression of utter contempt the next. If he's particularly good at

The directeurs *at La Coupole.*

his job of pleasing diners, it's the diners who end up trying to please him, ideally by ordering the aperitif, wine, and, yes, lobster he so elegantly and sincerely recommends. The surefire way to sell a special, according to Jean-Philippe Levasseur, La Coupole's most persuasive *maître d'hôtel*, is to float the idea of a dish "the chef has prepared especially for you" before the diner has had a chance to look at the menu. "No menu," he boasts, "can make it sound as good as I can."

The *directeur* and *directeur adjoint*, distinguished by dark business suits and long neckties, supervise the floor and help out wherever they're needed. They seat diners, answer telephones, clear tables, pour Champagne, assist with coat check, unsnarl traffic jams, expedite kitchen orders, check in on the indoor and sidewalk oyster stands, and keep tabs on the evening's lobster sales. Much of their time is consumed listening to the convoluted pleas of dejected and often indignant diners who show up either without reservations or thirty-plus minutes late for the ones they made. The *directeurs* tend to respond more patiently than you'd expect yet more firmly than the unseated diners would hope. A Parisian is entitled to an argument if not always a table.

Beneath the suave countenance of a *directeur* is a notoriously demanding boss capable of doing what few else in the history of brasseries have managed to do: make a *chef du rang* sweat. When I asked La Coupole's Claude Monteiro which of that brasserie's *directeurs* was the biggest pain in the ass he responded without hesitation: "*C'est moi.*"

THE BAR À VIN

You need to know what a bistro was to fully appreciate what a *bar à vin* is, namely a counter where you're served a glass of wine. Usually it is a *vin de propriété*, a wine purchased directly from the producer. Sometimes it is served with something to eat. That's it. As a surprisingly recent and still somewhat trendy distinction, the *bar à vin* or "wine bar" (it was fashionable back in the 1980s to use its English name) drives a good number of bistro owners crazy. The way they see it, the barmen *à vin* are claiming as

their own an essential service the Auvergnats introduced some 125 years before and the Parisians are falling for it.

The "bar-with-wine" hardly began with the bistro, as mentioned earlier. Wine-pouring French taverns go back two thousand years. The Defarge wineshop portrayed by Charles Dickens in *A Tale of Two Cities* resembles modern-era *bars à vin* like Rubis and Le Baron Rouge, right down to the bantering habitués, mistrusted newcomers, and nosy proprietors. There are things that even revolutions do not change. French cabarets operated wine bars, too.

As the bistros evolved into sit-down restaurants, demanding their patrons actually eat something, an opening was created for establishments that put wine consumption front and center, right and left. From the 1950s until the 1980s, the overwhelming majority of Parisian *bars à vin* were informal *comptoirs* (literally: counters) specializing in wines from a particular region, usually Beaujolais or the Loire Valley. Wines were invariably identified by the appellation indicating their origin but not their producer or vintage. You ordered a Saumur Champigny (a Loire red) but not a Saumur Champigny from so-and-so winemaker and so-and-so year. The owner of the *comptoir* thus got full credit or blame for his selection of nameless wines.

For food the *comptoirs* offered little more than cheeses, pâtés, charcuterie, and bread. Greens, fish, poultry, sweets, and fruit, save for crushed and fermented grapes and the odd ramekin of olives, were unheard of. Some eventually expanded their rations to include quiches, omelets, salads, or a *plat du jour*. Others turned themselves into *bistrots à vin*, a reinvention that probably did not amuse the Auvergnats all that much. The wine bar did not, however, prepare much that you would consider featuring in a cookbook.

That changed with the opening of L'Écluse on the site of the famous Left Bank cabaret in 1978 and Willi's Wine Bar in 1980. Each took food and, more importantly, the relationship between food and wine more seriously. Cheese and charcuterie alone would not cut it anymore. Each identified its wines by the producer and the year, an accurate reflection of a more comprehensive approach to wine selection and presentation. L'Écluse, an advocate of Bordeaux wines, has since cloned itself to become Paris's first wine bar chain. There are six of them. The one and only Willi's is still that, though its owner opened and then sold his interest in a second wine bar, Juvéniles, and took over a nearby restaurant he renamed Macéo.

Those unaware of Willi's opening date may be surprised to discover that its founder, Mark "Willi" Williamson, is still alive, much less that he is middle-aged and, like a tannic red wine, capable of further maturation. The world renown of his wine bar, supported in part by the retro art posters he's commissioned over the years to promote it, gives the impression of an enduring classic and, behind it, a legend among Parisian expats from the days of singer-dancer Josephine

Baker and novelist Henry Miller. But Willi is in fact an Englishman who's only scoured the French countryside since the 1980s, looking beyond the Beaujolais and Loire Valley wines favored by the *comptoirs* and past the aristocratic Burgundies and Bordeaux for unheralded alternatives. He's been a great champion of Rhone Valley wines and an unbending adversary of rosés. Plus, his Bar Mix (page 25) of fried leeks, potatoes, and zucchini is fabulous.

The rough model for a new generation of wine bars was introduced at Le Verre Volé, opened by Cyril Bordarier in 2000, and neatened up three years later by La Muse Vin, a more spacious, better-equipped imitator with a real kitchen. Le Verre Volé prepares its meals using toaster ovens and a steam cooker and depends on good ingredients to make up for the absence of a stove. Bordarier's concept was an extremely informal and cramped wine boutique/ *bar à vin* where diners could examine the wine bottles displayed on the shop walls, choose one, and pay a modest corkage fee of 5 euros (about $6.50 at this writing) no matter the wine's retail price. Bistros and restaurants generally charge two to three times the retail price for bottles.

Le Verre Volé is routinely packed for dinner. The bobos—bourgeois bohemians—appreciate its emphasis on organic wines, a few of them sulfite-free. Even so, Bordarier complains he is not making out all that well. His wine-pricing strategy is not working out as planned. Diners are choosing the cheapest wines and thus passing up what he correctly regards as the biggest bargains. They're taking 5-euro bottles and paying 10 euros, more or less what any restaurant would charge, when they could be taking 30-euro and 40-euro wines that, with the small corkage fee, sell for 35 and 45 euros respectively, at least half the amount a restaurant would typically charge.

"They're not playing the game," laments Bordarier.

Because this is first and foremost a cookbook, the wine bars it features were chosen on the basis of their cooking and their bar snacks and not their wine lists and cellars. As such, I do not claim that the wine bars listed here are by any means the best in Paris. Several great ones were left out, usually for want of hot food. Oenophiles would, however, find something interesting to drink in any of the *bars à vin* represented. Each has a distinctive approach to wine selection, and I encourage you to try them when visiting Paris.

The lists of featured extraordinary bistros and quintessential brasseries are not technically "best of" compilations either. They too consist of very personal choices singled out for their cuisine, the adaptability and doability of their chefs' recipes, and how they reflect in various ways what Parisians are eating now. All are truly extraordinary for the many ways in which they exalt the ordinary and make the City of Light the best place in the world to eat on a Tuesday night.

Hors d'œuvres and Snacks

HORS-D'ŒUVRE
ET SNACKS

CHEESE PUFFS

◦ GOUGÈRES ◦

MAKES 30 TO 35 PUFFS

Choux Pastry (recipe follows)

⅓ pound Comté, Gruyère, or Emmentaler, cut into ¼-inch cubes

½ teaspoon freshly ground black pepper

1 egg

The only truly convincing argument to be made against offering these delectable cheese puffs every night as an hors d'oeuvre, as practiced both at the first-rate bistro Natacha and, more famously, across the Seine at the renowned restaurant Taillevent, is to serve them instead as an appetizer. All that's required to transform them into a satisfying starter is a side salad of mixed greens drizzled with vinaigrette.

1. Preheat the oven to 400°F. Line a baking sheet with parchment paper. Prepare the choux pastry. Add the cheese cubes and black pepper to the pastry and mix well so that the cheese is evenly distributed.

2. Form 1 to 1½-inch balls of dough in one of two ways: Either fill a pastry bag with the dough and pipe out balls onto the lined baking sheet at least an inch apart or accomplish the same by using one teaspoon to gather the pastry and another to push it onto the sheet. (Though round, uniformly sized balls are a commendable goal; irregularly shaped ones turn out just fine.) Beat the egg with a teaspoon of cold water and brush this egg wash over the top halves of the balls. Bake for 20 minutes, shut off the oven, and let them sit in the oven for an additional 10 minutes. Serve immediately.

CHOUX PASTRY
(pâte à choux)

....

6 tablespoons unsalted
butter

1 teaspoon salt

Small pinch of ground
nutmeg (for savory pastry
only)

1 teaspoon granulated sugar
(for dessert pastry only)

¼ teaspoon pure vanilla
extract (for dessert pastry
only)

1 cup plus 2 tablespoons
flour, sifted

4 large eggs, at room
temperature

The dough that puts the puff in cream puffs, choux pastry (or choux paste) bakes into delicately crisp, ethereal shells that can accommodate a variety of moist fillings. It is used in both savories, as required in these cheese puffs, as well as several classic dessert pastries, Chocolate Profiteroles (page 180) and Paris-Brest (page 178), chief among them.

Combine 1 cup water, the butter, salt, and either nutmeg for a savory pastry or sugar and vanilla for a sweet one in a large saucepan over medium-high heat and bring to a boil, stirring with a wooden spoon so that the melted butter dissolves. Turn off the heat, add all of the flour at once, and stir with a wooden spoon, scraping the sides of the saucepan, until fully incorporated. Turn the heat on to low and cook, stirring constantly, until the batter dries a little and stops sticking to the pan. Remove from the heat and add the eggs, one at a time, mixing vigorously until each egg is fully incorporated before adding the next.

MARINATED RED PEPPERS

◦ SALADE DE POIVRONS MARINÉS ◦

MAKES ABOUT 2 CUPS

2 pounds red bell peppers

10 anchovy fillets, chopped

¼ cup dry white wine

3 tablespoons white wine
   vinegar

2 tablespoons extra virgin
   olive oil

1 teaspoon sugar

Salt

Freshly ground black pepper

1 cup canned crushed
   tomatoes

The sweetness of the peppers, the pungency of the anchovies, and the crisp acidity of the white wine and vinegar merge so that you can't tell what's coming from where. You can prepare the marinated peppers in one of two ways: Either roast the peppers first, as instructed, or skip the first step, slice the peppers with the skins on (discarding the stem, seeds, and inner core), and proceed to step 2. The first method is sweeter and more typical of antipasto-style marinated peppers, but the second is crunchier and thus works better as a salad. If you can't choose between the two, compromise by roasting half the peppers. You'll get some of the sweetness and some crunchiness.

1. Preheat the broiler to high. To roast the peppers, arrange them on a broiler pan and broil the peppers about 3 inches from the heat, turning occasionally with tongs, just until the skins are blackened. Transfer to a plastic bag, twist it tightly shut, and let stand for 15 minutes. When cool enough to handle, pull off the charred peel with your fingers. Cut the peeled peppers into 2-inch strips, discarding the stems, seeds, and the pulpy inner core.

2. Combine the anchovies, wine, vinegar, olive oil, and sugar in a saucepan over medium heat and heat to just below a boil. Add the peppers, season to taste with salt (lightly, the anchovies are already salty) and pepper, lower the heat, and cook at a gentle simmer, stirring occasionally, for 15 minutes. Add the crushed tomatoes and cook, stirring occasionally, for an additional 3 to 5 minutes. Remove from the heat and let marinate for at least 2 hours. Serve or transfer to a container or jar, cover tightly, and refrigerate for up to 3 days. Remove the peppers from the refrigerator at least 1 hour before serving.

CORNMEAL CRISPS *with* OVEN-ROASTED TOMATOES *and* TAPENADE

◦ CROUSTILLANTS AUX TOMATES CONFITES ET TAPENADE ◦

MAKES 6 SERVINGS

3 plum tomatoes

2 garlic cloves

Salt

Freshly ground black pepper

Tiny pinch of sugar

4 tablespoons olive oil

Butter

¼ cup fine cornmeal

½ cup flour

1 cup heavy cream

2 tablespoons commercial tapenade, or substitute a blend of 2 tablespoons chopped black olives, 1 teaspoon drained capers, and 2 teaspoons olive oil

2 teaspoons chopped basil

Great alone or with a variety of dips, these cornmeal crisps are flavored with oven-roasted tomatoes and tapenade, a paste of black olives, anchovies, and capers. You may add and substitute any number of finely chopped fillings (sun-dried tomatoes, onions, olives, fine herbs, fine chile pepper or roasted bell pepper). They're great, too, with sesame seeds or Parmesan cheese. These chips also form the foundation for Philippe Tredgeu's triple-decker Spring Vegetable Napoleon (page 41) or what I would call a napoleon of leftovers: Layer these crisps with Salt Cod and Avocado Brandade with Fresh Cilantro (page 61), Hachis Parmentier (page 105), Veal Blanquette (page 112), Celery Root Puree (page 131), stuffed Brie (page 158), or Lamb-Stuffed Eggplant Parmesan (page 118).

1. Preheat the oven to 200°F. To peel the tomatoes, cut a small X in the non-stem ends and plunge into boiling salted water for 30 seconds. Remove with a slotted spoon, place in ice water, drain, and peel. Cut each into 5 or 6 sections and remove the seeds.

2. Slice the garlic in half and place on the bottom of a nonstick baking pan. Place the tomato sections over the garlic, season with salt, pepper, and a tiny pinch of sugar, drizzle with 1 tablespoon olive oil, and cook in the oven for 1 hour.

3. Raise the oven temperature to 350°F and butter a large baking sheet. Combine the cornmeal, flour, cream, ½ teaspoon salt, and a few twists of freshly ground black pepper in a mixing bowl and beat with a whisk until smooth and fully blended. Add the oven-roasted tomatoes, the tapenade, and basil and mix until incorporated. Work-

ing in batches, spoon ¼ to ½ cup of the batter onto the prepared baking pan and spread and flatten it out with a spatula to an extremely thin layer. (You should almost be able to see the pan under the batter.) Add and spread out some more batter if it does not cover most of the pan. Use a sharp paring knife to cut that layer into rectangles of roughly equal size, about 2½ × 3½ inches each. Place in the oven, bake for 3 minutes, and check to see if the batter has spilled into the lines dividing the rectangles. If it has, delicately recut those areas. Bake until brown and crisp, about 15 minutes. Remove from the oven, let cool a few minutes, and delicately transfer each piece from the pan to a plate with a spatula. Repeat until all the batter has been used up. Serve or store in an airtight container.

BAR MIX

MAKES 4 TO 6 SERVINGS

2 leeks, white parts only

1 pound Idaho russet or Yukon gold potatoes, peeled

1 pound zucchini

½ cup flour

Salt

Peanut oil or vegetable oil, for frying

Forget foie gras. Abdicate caviar. Willi's Wine Bar eschews those snooty snacks for its Bar Mix, a messy tangle of fried potatoes, zucchini, and, most crucially, leeks. More than a fill-in for potato chips or peanuts, the Bar Mix is one way owner Mark Williamson makes wine tasting and appreciation accessible and fun.

1. Julienne the leeks and potatoes into spaghetti-thin strips. Wash them separately in cold water, drain, and thoroughly pat dry.

2. Slice the zucchini into thin rounds no thicker than ⅛ inch. Combine them in a bowl with the flour and a little salt and toss to coat.

3. Clip a deep-frying thermometer to the side of a deep, heavy-bottomed saucepan. Heat 3 inches of oil over high heat to 350°F. Fry the leeks until browned, 2 to 3 minutes. Remove with a slotted spoon, drain on paper towels, and sprinkle with salt. Repeat with the potatoes, frying them until golden brown, 4 to 5 minutes. Finally, fry the zucchini until browned, 3 to 4 minutes. Toss the fried vegetables together and serve in a napkin-lined bowl or basket.

EGGPLANT TAPENADE

∘ TAPENADE D'AUBERGINE ∘

MAKES 2 CUPS

1 large eggplant, about
   1 pound

Extra virgin olive oil

Salt

1/2 cup oil-packed sun-dried
   tomatoes, coarsely chopped

1/2 cup coarsely chopped
   pitted black olives

2 teaspoons drained capers

1/4 to 1/2 teaspoon piment
   d'Espelette or ancho
   powder or other medium-
   hot chili powder, optional

Freshly ground black pepper

1 baguette, thinly sliced and
   toasted

The house dip at the wine bar Juvéniles is a tapenade, the Provençal paste of black olives, capers, and olive oil, doctored with baked eggplant, sun-dried tomatoes, and, for added zip, piment d'Espelette. Serve as you would a traditional tapenade; either spread over toasts (or pita triangles, crackers, or bagel chips) or as a condiment with boiled potatoes, fresh tomatoes, or fish. When it is served as an hors d'oeuvre, owner Tim Johnston suggests matching its pungent flavors to a young, fruity, lightly chilled Beaujolais.

1. Preheat the oven to 375°F. Peel the eggplant and slice into 1/2-inch rounds. Brush the rounds on both sides with olive oil, sprinkle with salt, arrange the rounds in a single layer on the bottom of a large baking pan, and bake until soft, 30 to 40 minutes.

2. Place the eggplant in a food processor, add the sun-dried tomatoes, olives, capers, 1/3 cup olive oil, piment d'Espelette, and a few twists of freshly ground black pepper and puree to a paste, about 30 seconds. Correct the seasoning and serve with toasted baguette slices.

Piment d'Espelette

....

Piment d'Espelette is the hottest spice in Paris, in part because it's not all that hot. The famous chile pepper from ten communes in France's Basque region, including the village of Espelette, rates a medium 4 on the Scoville heat scale as compared to a 5 for jalapeños, an 8 for cayenne peppers, and a deadly 10 out of 10 for habaneros. As such, the piquant, medium-hot powder from the piment d'Espelette spices up a dish without overpowering it, a concern that scares many French chefs away from hot chile peppers. A conically shaped red chile pepper 3 to 5 inches long with a rounded point, the piment d'Espelette is also prized for a lingering fruity aroma not found in other chiles. Its origin and cultivation are controlled by an AOC (*appellation d'origine contrôlée*) designation, the same classification that protects the good names of fine French wines and cheeses.

Piment d'Espelette may be purchased at gourmet food stores or ordered from www.chefshop.com and www.purespice.com. As a substitute, I've suggested ancho chili powder. Cayenne pepper is too hot and would need to be diluted by a milder chili powder or paprika or used in smaller quantities.

....

DEEP-FRIED VEGETABLES

◦ FRITURE DE LÉGUMES ◦

MAKES 4 TO 6 SERVINGS

1 zucchini

2 baby eggplant, peeled

2 beets, peeled

1 carrot, peeled

1 leek, white parts only

1½ cups fine semolina flour

2 teaspoons salt

¼ teaspoon piment
  d'Espelette or ancho
  powder or other medium-
  hot chili powder

Peanut oil, for frying

Lemon wedges

Fresh mint sprigs

Tartar Sauce (page 29),
  optional

This hors d'oeuvre reflects a move away from heavy, puffy, batter-fried beignets to floured, lightly crisp fried vegetables in the tempura mold. You can prepare it with any combination and quantity of vegetables. The same semolina-flour coating makes terrific fried calamari, too.

1. Use a mandolin or sharp knife to cut the zucchini, eggplant, beets, and carrot into the thinnest rounds possible. Wash and pat dry the leek and cut into a julienne.

2. Sift together the semolina flour and salt in a bowl, season with piment d'Espelette, add the vegetables, and toss to coat.

3. Clip a deep-frying thermometer to the side of a heavy-bottomed saucepan. Heat 3 inches of oil over high heat to 360°F. Lift the vegetables from the semolina, shaking off any excess, and fry in small batches until golden brown, about 3 minutes. Drain on paper towels. Serve with lemon wedges, fresh mint sprigs, and, if desired, tartar sauce.

TARTAR SAUCE

◦ SAUCE TARTARE ◦

MAKES 2 CUPS

1½ cups Classic
Mayonnaise (page 31)

2 tablespoons drained
capers

2 tablespoons minced
shallots

3 gherkins or 1 small sweet
pickle, finely chopped

1 tablespoon chopped fresh
tarragon

1 tablespoon chopped fresh
parsley

1 tablespoon chopped chives

1 dash (about 5 drops)
Tabasco sauce or
substitute 1 pinch piment
d'Espelette or
cayenne pepper

Salt

Freshly ground black pepper

*Thierry Faucher prepares this classic tartar sauce, which is so much
better than the stuff you get in a jar, as one of several dips served
with his wine bar's mixed crudités (page 30). It is also a great
accompaniment for the Sesame Salmon Fingers (page 60) and
Mackerel Croquettes (page 63).*

Place the mayonnaise in a mixing bowl. Finely chop the capers and
add to the mayonnaise along with the shallots, gherkins, tarragon,
parsley, and chives. Season with Tabasco sauce, salt, and pepper and
mix well. Cover and refrigerate for at least 2 hours and up to 3 days.

CRUDITÉS *with* THREE DIPS

◦ PANIER DE LÉGUMES ◦

1 cucumber

1 red bell pepper

1 green bell pepper

2 cups cherry tomatoes

2 cups cauliflower florets

3 carrots, peeled and cut into sticks

1 zucchini, cut into sticks or diagonal slices

1 bunch radishes, cleaned and trimmed

4 to 5 white mushrooms, cleaned and sliced

1/2 cup Tartar Sauce (page 29)

1/2 cup Basil and Black Olive Mayonnaise (page 31)

1/2 cup Piment d'Espelette Mayonnaise (page 31)

Serve this wine bar's basket of mixed raw vegetables with three dips: a classic tartar sauce and two flavored mayonnaises, one with black olives and basil, the other with piment d'Espelette, as suggested, or others of your choice.

1. Peel the cucumber, cut in half lengthwise, scoop out the seeds, and cut into sticks.

2. Cut around the stems of the bell peppers and remove them. Cut the peppers in half lengthwise, clean out the core and seeds, and cut into thin strips.

3. Arrange all the vegetables on a large serving plate or in a basket. Serve with tartar sauce and two flavored mayonnaises.

Classic Mayonnaise

MAKES ABOUT 1 CUP

2 egg yolks, beaten

1 teaspoon Dijon mustard

Pinch of salt

Freshly ground black pepper

1 teaspoon white wine
vinegar

1 cup fresh vegetable oil,
such as canola, soybean,
corn, sunflower, or light
olive

This recipe and its flavored variations are inspired by the dips served at the wine bar La Cave à l'Os à Moelle.

1. Bring the ingredients to room temperature (about 30 minutes out of the refrigerator).

2. Put the beaten yolks, mustard, salt, and pepper in a round-bottomed mixing bowl, always resting it on a flat surface, and beat with a whisk until blended and pale yellow in color. Add the vinegar and beat quickly until fully incorporated. Very slowly add the oil, drop by drop, beating vigorously with the whisk, until an emulsion forms and the sauce thickens. Add the rest of the oil, little by little, beating continuously. Serve immediately or cover and refrigerate for up to 5 days.

Basil and Black Olive Mayonnaise: Blanch ¼ cup basil leaves in boiling salted water for 30 seconds, drain, plunge into cold water, drain again, and pat dry. Finely chop the basil and blend into the mayonnaise with ¼ cup chopped pitted black olives.

Piment d'Espelette Mayonnaise: Blend ½ to 1 teaspoon piment d'Espelette into the mayonnaise.

Tarragon Mayonnaise: Blend 3 tablespoons chopped fresh tarragon and 1 tablespoon fresh lemon juice into the mayonnaise.

TOMATO TOAST

⚬ PAIN À LA TOMATE ⚬

MAKES 6 TO 8 SERVINGS

1 French country bread or
   baguette, cut into ½ to
   ¾-inch slices

3 garlic cloves, halved

4 to 5 plum tomatoes,
   halved

¼ cup extra virgin olive oil

Coarse sea salt

¼ pound Serrano ham, or
   other fine cured ham,
   thinly sliced, optional

Chef-owner Didier Oudill serves these garlic-and tomato-rubbed toasts, a Catalan specialty known in Catalonia as pa amb tomaquet *and in parts of France as* pain à la tomate, *with all his bistro's* parrilladas *(Spanish for "mixed grills"), including one featuring market vegetables (page 124). They are equally good as an hors d'oeuvre or salad accompaniment.*

Grill or toast the bread slices on both sides and then, if using bread from a round loaf, cut into smaller slices 2 to 3 inches wide. Rub one side of the toasts with the cut garlic and then with the flat sides of the tomato halves, mashing the tomatoes so that the juice, pulp, and seeds are soaked into the toast. Drizzle with olive oil, sprinkle with salt, and top, if desired, with a slice of Serrano ham. Serve warm or at room temperature.

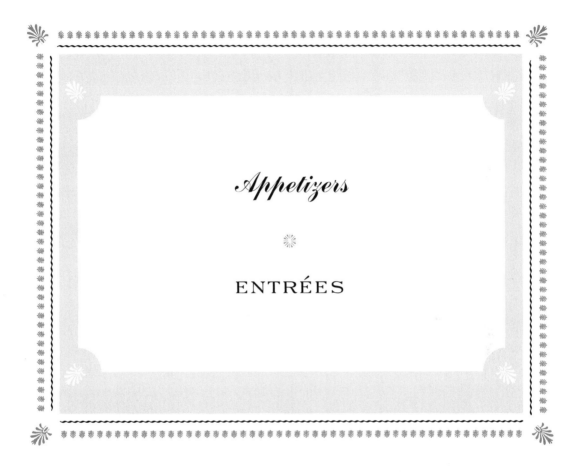

Appetizers

ENTRÉES

ENDIVE TATIN *with* GOAT CHEESE

◦ TATIN D'ENDIVES AU CHÈVRE ◦

MAKES 4 SERVINGS

12 tablespoons (1½ sticks)
   unsalted butter, at room
   temperature

½ cup potato flour

1 cup flour

Salt

3 egg yolks

3 pounds Belgian endive

2 tablespoons lemon juice

½ cup sugar

¼ pound goat cheese,
   crumbled

⅓ cup honey

2 teaspoons sherry

1 teaspoon Dijon mustard

1 teaspoon coriander seeds,
   crushed

3 tablespoons olive oil

François Pasteau created what has become his signature dish for the millions of Frenchmen who grew up detesting the bitter, watery, cooked-to-death Belgian endive their parents forced upon them. Already adept at blurring the distinction between sweet and savory at his Left Bank bistro, Pasteau patterned this appetizer after a dessert classic that constitutes one of the fondest memories of a French childhood, the tarte Tatin *(upside-down caramelized apple tart).*

1. To prepare the pastry: Place 6 tablespoons butter in a large mixing bowl. Gradually add the potato flour, mixing it into the butter until fully incorporated. Do the same with the flour and a pinch of salt. Add the egg yolks, one at a time, mixing vigorously until they are fully incorporated. Add 1 teaspoon water and mix until the dough is homogeneous. Roll the dough into a smooth compact ball, place it in a bowl, cover with a damp cloth, and refrigerate for at least 1 hour and up to 24 hours.

2. Discard the bruised leaves of the endive. Remove their bitter conical cores with the tip of a paring knife and discard. Separate the leaves of the endive and place them in a pot of boiling salted water. Add the lemon juice and boil for 30 minutes. Drain the endive thoroughly and set aside.

3. Preheat the oven to 350°F. Melt the remaining 6 tablespoons butter in a saucepan over medium heat. Add the sugar and cook, stirring continuously with a wooden spoon, until the mixture thickens into a creamy caramel (the mixture will first harden and then separate before it reunites and turns creamy). Pour into a 9 to 10-inch pie tin and quickly spread it in an even layer before it hardens. Let cool for a few minutes.

4. Arrange the endive in even layers over the caramel and then top with an even layer of crumbled goat cheese.

5. Using a rolling pin, carefully roll out the dough on a lightly floured work surface to a thickness of ¼ to ⅓ inch and cut or trim it into a circle slightly larger than the pie pan. Place the circle over the pan and press the overlapping border into the interior rim of the pan. Bake until the top is lightly golden but not browned, 20 minutes.

6. Heat the honey, sherry, mustard, crushed coriander seeds, and ¼ cup water in a saucepan over medium heat just to a boil. Lower the heat to very low and gently simmer for 5 minutes. Just before serving, add the olive oil to the simmering sauce and beat with a whisk.

7. To serve, turn the tart over a serving plate (it will unmold easily). Slice into wedges and spoon the honey sauce over and around each serving.

PAN-FRIED GOAT CHEESE SALAD *with* HAZELNUT VINAIGRETTE

◦ SALADE DE CHÈVRE PANÉ À L'HUILE DE NOISETTE ◦

MAKES 4 SERVINGS

6 ounces goat cheese

1 egg, beaten

4 tablespoons peanut oil

½ cup bread crumbs

Salt

Freshly ground black pepper

3 tablespoons unsalted
butter

1 tablespoon balsamic
vinegar, plus 2 teaspoons
for garnish

2 tablespoons olive oil

1 tablespoon hazelnut oil

4 to 6 cups mesclun or
mixed salad greens (frisée,
arugula, escarole, mustard
greens, endive)

¼ cup chopped walnuts

¼ cup fresh chives, cut into
1-inch lengths

By pan-frying the breaded goat cheese rounds in a combination of butter and oil you get the sweet flavor of the butter and the higher frying temperature of the oil. There is plenty of flexibility in the use and quantity of nuts and nut oils. For example, substitute walnut oil for the hazelnut oil, increase the amount of either, or add ground nuts to the bread crumbs to make the goat cheese crunchier.

1. Carefully slice the goat cheese into 12 small rounds about ⅓ inch thick.

2. Combine the egg, 1 tablespoon peanut oil, and 1 tablespoon cold water in a bowl and mix with a whisk. Spread the bread crumbs over a plate and season with salt and pepper. Dunk the cheese rounds, one at a time, into the egg mixture, letting the excess drip back into the bowl, then roll in the bread crumbs to fully coat on both sides. Refrigerate the breaded goat cheese rounds for about 15 minutes.

3. Heat the butter and the remaining 3 tablespoons peanut oil in a skillet over medium-high heat. Carefully place the breaded goat cheese rounds in the pan and fry until light brown, 2 to 3 minutes on each side. Drain on paper towels.

4. For the vinaigrette: Place 1 tablespoon vinegar in a bowl, season with salt and pepper, and slowly beat in the olive oil and hazelnut oil.

5. To serve, combine the salad greens, vinaigrette, and chopped walnuts in a bowl. Place a small mound of salad greens in the center of four plates, surround each with 3 goat cheese rounds, drizzle the outside of the plate with balsamic vinegar, and garnish with the cut chives.

SLICED ZUCCHINI *with* LEMON ZEST *and* FRESH GOAT CHEESE

◦ ÉMINCÉ DE COURGETTE AU ZESTE DE CITRON ET CHÈVRE FRAIS ◦

MAKES 4 SERVINGS

1 green zucchini

1 yellow zucchini or other yellow summer squash

6 ounces goat cheese, crumbled

¼ cup olive oil

Zest and juice of 1 lemon

2 teaspoons finely chopped fresh mint

Coarse sea salt

Freshly ground black pepper

Initially, this recipe doesn't read any more impressively on Le Rouge-Gorge's wine bar menu than it does here. But the thinly sliced raw zucchini has a nice crunch, and the combination of lemon zest, olive oil, and fresh goat cheese is light, refreshing, and delightful. This is a great summer appetizer when you don't have the time or energy to fuss.

Using a mandolin or sharp knife, slice the zucchini into extremely thin rounds. Place the goat cheese on four plates and top with a layer of zucchini rounds. Drizzle with olive oil and lemon juice, sprinkle with the zest and mint, and season with salt and pepper.

SPRING VEGETABLE NAPOLEON

◦ CROUSTILLANT DE PETITS LÉGUMES ◦

MAKES 6 SERVINGS

1 pound baby carrots,
   peeled, or substitute 2 to 3
   large carrots cut into
   3-inch sticks

1 cup shelled fresh peas

½ pound haricots verts or
   thin string beans, ends
   clipped

1 cup shelled fava beans

½ cup cherry tomatoes,
   halved

2 tablespoons white wine

2 shallots, thinly sliced

2 tablespoons red wine
   vinegar

2 tablespoons balsamic
   vinegar

2 tablespoons olive oil

¼ cup vegetable oil

Salt

Freshly ground black pepper

Cornmeal Crisps
   (page 23)

In this savory napoleon, spring vegetables are boiled until crisp-tender, drizzled with a crisp vinaigrette, and layered between the cornmeal crisps of Philippe Tredgeu's triple-decker croustillant, which, if it's not already obvious, is French for "crisp." Pencil-thin asparagus, when available and in season, are a splendid addition: Cut the woody sections off the bottoms and discard, boil in salted water just until they may be penetrated with a knife (3 to 6 minutes, depending on their thickness), drain, and plunge into ice water. The vinaigrette, neither too acidic nor too sweet, is great for saucing boiled or steamed vegetables.

1. Cook the carrots, peas, haricots verts, and fava beans separately in boiling salted water just until slightly tender, about 4 minutes for the carrots and haricots verts and 5 minutes for the peas and fava beans. Plunge each into ice water to stop the cooking process and set in the color. Drain. Once the fava beans have cooled, peel off their white skins by pinching through the skin opposite the growing tip. Place the cooked vegetables and the halved cherry tomatoes in a salad bowl.

2. Prepare the vinaigrette: Combine the wine and shallots in a saucepan over moderately high heat and cook until all the wine has evaporated, about 2 minutes. Add the two vinegars and remove from the heat. Add the two oils, season with salt and pepper, and beat with a whisk until blended. Pour the vinaigrette over the vegetables and toss.

3. To serve, place a crisp on the bottom of six plates. Top with a layer of vegetables about ¾ inch thick, another crisp, another layer of vegetables, and finally a third crisp.

COLD VEGETABLE SALAD *with* FRESH CORIANDER

◦ SALADE DE LÉGUMES À LA CORIANDRE FRAÎCHE ◦

MAKES 6 SERVINGS

3 carrots, peeled and cut into sticks

1 fennel bulb, thickly sliced

2 celery stalks, cut into 1-inch slices

1 small head cauliflower, cut into 1-inch florets or chunks

2 tablespoons olive oil

2 teaspoons coriander seeds

3 garlic cloves, chopped

½ cup dry white wine

3 cups chicken stock

1 cup sweet white wine, such as Sauterne or Riesling

Salt

Freshly ground black pepper

½ teaspoon piment d'Espelette or ancho powder or other medium-hot chili powder, optional

3 tablespoons red wine vinegar

The dried seeds and fresh leaves of the coriander plant are of equal importance in Thierry Blanqui's cold cooked vegetable salad. The seeds gradually impart their citrusy, gently spicy aroma to the vegetables as they are sautéed, simmered, and, in effect, pickled. The fresh leaves (cilantro), a last-second garnish, punctuate the salad with a zap of their pungent perfume, which perks up the vegetables. The choice of vegetables is flexible and varies at this bistro according to season and market availability. Possible substitutions include asparagus, haricots verts (or slender green beans), Jerusalem artichokes, and shelled fava beans.

1. Blanch each vegetable separately in boiling salted water for 2 minutes, drain, plunge into cold water to stop the cooking process and set in the color, drain again, and pat dry.

2. Heat the olive oil in a saucepan over medium heat, add the coriander seeds and garlic, and cook, stirring once or twice, for 2 minutes. Add the carrots and cook for 4 minutes. Add the fennel and celery and cook until they become slightly tender, 4 to 6 minutes. Pour in the dry white wine to deglaze the pan. Quickly add the chicken stock, sweet white wine, and cauliflower, season with salt, pepper, and, if desired, piment d'Espelette, and cook at a slow simmer until crisp-tender, 12 to 15 minutes. Remove from the heat, immediately add the vinegar to halt the cooking, and let cool.

3. If adding bacon, cook it in a skillet over medium heat just until it begins to crisp, about 4 minutes. Drain on paper towels and add to the vegetables.

*3 to 4 strips bacon, diced,
optional*

*1/2 cup chopped fresh
cilantro*

4. Correct the seasoning, transfer the vegetables with their liquid to a bowl or container, cover with plastic wrap, and let marinate in the refrigerator for at least 12 hours and up to 5 days. To serve, remove the vegetables with a slotted spoon, drizzle some of the marinade over them, and sprinkle with fresh cilantro.

TERRINE OF SLOW-ROASTED VEGETABLES *with* FLEUR DE SEL DE GUÉRANDE

◦ TERRINE DE LÉGUMES CONFIT AU SEL DE GUÉRANDE ◦

MAKES 8 TO 10 SERVINGS

One ½-pound eggplant

Salt

1 cup olive oil

Freshly ground black pepper

4 medium tomatoes

1 teaspoon chopped fresh thyme

1 teaspoon chopped fresh cilantro

4 garlic cloves, chopped

1 bay leaf

2 medium red bell peppers

1 fennel bulb, peeled and thinly sliced

2 medium zucchini, thinly sliced

One ¼-ounce envelope unflavored gelatin

½ cup tomato juice

Fleur de sel de Guérande or substitute coarse sea salt

Balsamic vinegar

In this brasserie's vegetable terrine, served as you would a pâté, the fleur de sel enhances the flavors of the slow-roasted vegetables after they've been cooked.

1. Cut the eggplant into ¼-inch-thick rounds, sprinkle with salt, set aside for 30 minutes, and pat dry. Preheat the oven to 325°F. Brush a sheet pan with a little olive oil, arrange the eggplant rounds in a single layer in the pan, drizzle with olive oil, season with pepper, and bake in the oven until tender, about 45 minutes.

2. While the eggplant is baking, peel the tomatoes: Cut a small X in the non-stem ends, plunge into boiling salted water for 30 seconds, drain, plunge into cold water, and peel. Cut each tomato into thin sections, combine in a bowl with ½ teaspoon chopped thyme, ½ teaspoon chopped cilantro, 2 chopped garlic cloves, the bay leaf, and 2 tablespoons olive oil, season with salt and pepper, and mix well. Spoon the tomato mixture into a nonstick baking pan and bake, turning occasionally, until very soft, about 1 hour. Remove the bay leaf.

3. Arrange the bell peppers directly over a gas burner on high. Roast the peppers, turning every couple of minutes with a pair of tongs, until thoroughly charred. Place the peppers in a plastic bag for 10 minutes to loosen the skins. Rub off the skins with your fingers, open up the peppers, scrape out the seeds, and cut into ½-inch-wide slices.

Flat-leaf parsley, for garnish
1 baguette, sliced and
toasted

4. Heat ¼ cup olive oil in a saucepan over medium heat. Add the peppers, fennel, zucchini, and the remaining chopped garlic, thyme, and cilantro, season with salt and pepper, and cook for 2 minutes. Lower the heat to very low and cook, stirring occasionally, until very soft, about 1 hour. Remove the vegetables with a slotted spoon, leaving any liquid in the saucepan.

5. Sprinkle the gelatin over ¼ cup water in a small bowl, stir, and let stand for 5 minutes.

6. Add the tomato juice to the vegetable juices in the saucepan and heat over medium heat until the liquid steams but does not boil. Stir in the dissolved gelatin and remove from heat.

7. Rinse the inside of an 8 × 4 × 2½-inch loaf pan or terrine pan with cold water, leaving its inside surface wet. Line the pan with plastic wrap, leaving enough to overlap the edges by at least 4 inches. Place half the eggplant rounds in an even layer on the bottom of the pan, sprinkle with fleur de sel, season with pepper, and pour about a quarter of the liquid gelatin mixture (¼ to ⅓ cup) over the eggplant. Top that layer with an even layer of the pepper, zucchini, and fennel mixture, sprinkle with fleur de sel, season with pepper, and cover with another ¼ to ⅓ cup of the liquid gelatin mixture. Press down gently on the vegetables as you build the terrine. Do the same with a layer of the remaining tomatoes, then finally a layer of eggplant, and sprinkle with fleur de sel. Press down one last time, pour just enough of the liquid gelatin mixture into the pan to fill the gaps between the vegetables, close the plastic wrap over the terrine, pressing the plastic down into the terrine, and refrigerate for at least 6 hours and up to 2 days.

8. To serve, peel back the plastic wrap covering the terrine, turn the terrine out on a platter or serving dish, and unmold by delicately lifting up the pan while holding down the exposed plastic wrap. Peel off the plastic wrap and carefully cut the terrine into 1-inch slices with a serrated knife. Drizzle each slice with olive oil and balsamic vinegar, sprinkle with fleur de sel, and garnish with parsley. Serve with the toasted baguette slices.

Fleur de Sel de Guérande

....

Naturally harvested from lowland marshes around the town of Guérande in Brittany, fleur de sel de Guérande is a French sea salt prized by chefs for its texture, flavor, and purity. Its flaky crystals are crunchy, yet, because they retain moisture, melt easily in the mouth, releasing their mineral-rich, faintly bitter taste of the sea. Coarse fleur de sel is mostly used as a finishing salt for fish, meats, or vegetables at the last moment to draw out their flavors and add texture. The caviar of salt, as fleur de sel de Guérande is often revered, would be the first choice in any recipe in this book that calls for coarse sea salt, though French fleur de sel from Camargue, Ile de Re, and Noirmoutier are also excellent.

Fleur de sel de Guérande is sold in fine gourmet shops or may be ordered from www.chefshop.com and www.salt-works.us.

....

STEAMED WHOLE ARTICHOKES *with* POACHED EGG *and* VINAIGRETTE

◦ ARTICHAUTS À LA BRETONNE À L'ŒUF POCHÉ ET VINAIGRETTE ◦

MAKES 4 SERVINGS

4 large artichokes

1 large lemon, halved

1 tablespoon all-purpose flour

Salt

1/3 cup sherry vinegar

1 tablespoon Dijon mustard

2 tablespoons chopped fresh herbs, such as tarragon, chives, chervil, flat-leaf parsley

1 cup extra virgin olive oil

Freshly ground black pepper

1 tablespoon white wine vinegar

4 eggs

Your first reaction to this elemental bistro trio might be a puzzled "That's it?" But in season, a medium to large artichoke is a magnificent vegetable and a delight to deconstruct and dip in runny egg yolk and herb-infused vinaigrette. Anything more orchestral would just be a distraction.

1. Working with one artichoke at a time, break off and discard the stems, bend and snap off the bottom outer leaves at the base, and use scissors to trim off the top inch of the remaining leaves.

2. Combine the lemon, flour, 1 tablespoon salt, and 2 quarts water in a large pot and heat, stirring occasionally, to a boil. Add the artichokes, top with a plate to hold them down, lower the heat, and simmer, uncovered, until the leaves pull off easily, about 30 minutes. Remove the artichokes with a slotted spoon, drain them upside down in a colander, and cover to keep warm.

3. Prepare the vinaigrette: Combine the sherry vinegar, mustard, and herbs, season with salt, and mix with a whisk. Slowly whisk in the olive oil and season with pepper.

4. Pour 1½ to 2 inches of water into a large saucepan, add the vinegar, season with a little salt, and bring just to a boil. Break an egg into a cup, lower the tilted cup into the water, and slowly slide the egg into the water. Repeat with the remaining eggs, being careful to space them apart, lower the heat to the point where the water barely simmers, and poach until the whites are set but the yolks are still runny, about 3 minutes. Remove the eggs with a slotted spoon, smooth their surfaces by trimming off any rough residue of the whites with scissors, and drain on paper towels.

5. To serve, pull apart the first large leaves of each artichoke, pull out the interior leaves, plant an egg in the recess left by them, and season the egg with salt and pepper. Remix the vinaigrette, pour into four ramekins or small bowls, and serve the vinaigrette with the artichokes as a dip for the leaves.

STEAMED ASPARAGUS VINAIGRETTE *with* POACHED EGG *and* SERRANO HAM

◦ ASPERGES À LA VINAIGRETTE, ŒUF POCHÉ MOLLET, ET JAMBON SERRANO ◦

MAKES 4 SERVINGS

1½ pounds asparagus, trimmed

1 tablespoon plus 1 teaspoon sherry vinegar

1 teaspoon Dijon mustard

2 teaspoons chopped fresh chives

½ teaspoon salt

¼ cup extra virgin olive oil

Freshly ground black pepper

1 tablespoon white wine vinegar

4 eggs

4 thin slices serrano or other cured ham

1 French country bread or baguette, sliced and toasted

2 garlic cloves, halved

The more passionate the lover of fresh seasonal asparagus, the more basic his or her favorite recipe for it. Or so it seems, not only in a minimally equipped kitchenette like the one at Cyril Bordarier's wine bar but also in accomplished bistro and restaurant kitchens throughout Paris. Breaking the yolk of a poached egg over the steamed asparagus is the diner's prerogative as well as his or her reward.

1. Fill the bottom of a steamer with water and bring to a boil. Place the asparagus in the steamer basket, cover, and steam until bright green and just tender, 6 to 8 minutes.

2. Prepare the vinaigrette: Combine the sherry vinegar, mustard, chives, and salt and mix with a whisk. Slowly whisk in the olive oil and season with pepper.

3. Pour 1½ to 2 inches of water into a large saucepan, add the vinegar, season with a little salt, and bring just to a boil. Break an egg into a cup, lower the tilted cup into the water, and slowly slide the egg into the water. Repeat with the remaining eggs, being careful to space them apart, lower the heat to the point where the water barely simmers, and poach until the whites are set but the yolks are still runny, about 3 minutes. Remove the eggs with a slotted spoon, smooth their surfaces by trimming off the rough residue of the whites with scissors, and drain on paper towels.

4. To serve, remix the vinaigrette. Divide the asparagus among four plates, drizzle with vinaigrette, top each with a poached egg, and serve immediately with serrano ham and toast rubbed with garlic.

POACHED EGGS CORDON BLEU

○ LES ŒUFS MOLLETS CORDON BLEU ○

MAKES 4 SERVINGS

2 to 3 tablespoons white
 wine vinegar

Salt

11 eggs

3 ounces serrano ham or
 prosciutto, thinly sliced

4 ounces Gruyère or Swiss,
 thinly sliced

Vegetable oil, for frying

½ cup flour

1 cup bread crumbs

3 tablespoons extra virgin
 olive oil

1 tablespoon balsamic
 vinegar

2 to 3 cups trimmed and
 cleaned arugula leaves

Coarse sea salt

Freshly ground black pepper

When applied to the name of a dish, cordon bleu, *French for "blue ribbon," refers to veal or chicken that's been topped with or rolled in ham and Gruyère cheese, breaded, and fried. Here Michel Rostang applies the classic preparation to poached eggs, which, due to their softness, are more difficult to handle than meat. The reward is when you cut through the crisp breading to pierce the egg and spread the runny yolk over the ham, cheese, and arugula. If you do break a yolk while rolling a egg, do not panic. The result, comparable to a ham, cheese, and fried-egg sandwich, will still be delicious.*

1. Working in 2 or 3 batches and changing the poaching liquid if necessary, pour 1½ to 2 inches of water into a large saucepan, add 1 tablespoon vinegar, season with a little salt, and bring just to a boil. Break an egg into a cup, lower the tilted cup into the water, and slowly slide the egg into the water. Repeat with up to 3 more eggs, being careful to space them apart, lower the heat to the point where the water barely simmers, and poach until the whites are set but the yolks are still runny, about 3 minutes. Remove the eggs with a slotted spoon, smooth their surfaces by trimming off the rough residue of the whites with scissors, and drain on paper towels. Prepare additional batches until 8 eggs have been poached.

2. Beat the remaining 3 eggs with 1 tablespoon cold water. Cut the ham and cheese slices into 8 strips about the width of the poached eggs. Place a band of cheese over each band of ham.

3. Clip a deep-frying thermometer to the side of a large heavy-bottomed saucepan and heat 2 inches of oil over moderately high heat to 325°F. Working one at a time, delicately place a poached egg on the cheese and roll the egg in the ham and cheese, being careful not to crush the egg yolk. Holding the bundle together in your hands,

delicately roll it in the flour to coat all sides, shaking off the excess, then in the beaten egg mixture and bread crumbs. Lower the egg bundle into the oil and fry until golden, 1 to 2 minutes. Lift carefully with a slotted spoon and drain on paper towels.

4. To serve, gradually add the olive oil to the balsamic vinegar, mixing with a whisk. Divide the arugula leaves among four plates, drizzle with vinaigrette, season with salt and pepper, and top with the egg bundles (2 per serving).

Salad of Marinated Tuna Fillets with Roasted Vegetables and Olive Oil

◦ FILET DE THON MARINÉ À L'HUILE D'OLIVE, LÉGUMES DE SUD ◦

MAKES 4 TO 6 SERVINGS

1 pound tuna fillets,
  preferably bluefin or
  yellowfin (ahi)

4 tablespoons chopped fresh
  cilantro

2 garlic cloves, chopped

Pinch of cumin powder

Freshly squeezed juice of
  2 lemons (about 5
  tablespoons)

1/2 cup extra virgin olive oil

Salt

Freshly ground black pepper

4 plum tomatoes

2 onions, thinly sliced

1 red pepper, cored, seeded,
  and thinly sliced

1 fennel bulb, thinly sliced

French country bread or
  baguette, sliced and
  toasted

An appealing departure from routine salads made with canned or grilled tuna, this wine bar's version combines marinated strips of fresh tuna, crisp tender vegetables, and a garlicky, cilantro-scented olive oil marinade. It can be prepared days in advance and served as a dinner appetizer, lunch dish, or picnic salad.

1. Cut the tuna into thin, 1-inch-wide strips, place in a bowl, cover with 2 tablespoons chopped cilantro, the garlic, cumin, lemon juice, and olive oil, season generously with salt and pepper, and let marinate for 20 minutes at room temperature.

2. Preheat the oven to 400°F. To peel the tomatoes, cut a small X in the non-stem ends and plunge into boiling salted water for 30 seconds. Remove with a slotted spoon, place in ice water, drain, peel, and cut into thin slices.

3. Place all of the onion slices on the bottom of a 9 by 13-inch baking dish (or the equivalent). Top with the red pepper, fennel, and tomatoes. Place the tuna strips in an even layer over the vegetables, top with the marinade, and bake for 10 minutes for medium rare tuna, 15 minutes for tuna that is cooked through. Remove from the oven, let cool, cover with plastic wrap, and refrigerate for at least 2 hours and up to 4 days. Just before serving, sprinkle with the remaining chopped cilantro and serve with the toast.

COLD TUNA *and* SPRING VEGETABLES IN A JAR

◦ RECUITE DE THON PRINTANIÈRE EN BOCAL ◦

MAKES 4 APPETIZER
SERVINGS OR 8 HORS
D'OEUVRE SERVINGS

2 medium eggplant (1¼ to
  1½ pounds total)

1 teaspoon sugar

2 teaspoons fresh chopped
  thyme

Salt

Freshly ground black pepper

6 tablespoons extra virgin
  olive oil

2 garlic cloves

2 medium tomatoes, diced

2 roasted bell peppers, diced
  (see page 22)

4 anchovy fillets, chopped

1 tablespoon chopped fresh
  basil

2 teaspoons red wine
  vinegar

6 ounces canned or jarred
  white tuna fillets in oil

8 to 10 small black olives

6 to 8 arugula leaves,
  trimmed and cleaned

8 slices country bread, toasted

Le Dauphin was among the first Parisian bistros to assemble terrines, salads, pâtés, and various combination cold appetizers in Mason jars and later serve them with toast as you would conserves. Each jar may be served as a shared appetizer or hors d'oeuvre. This Provençal combination of tuna, roasted eggplant, tomato, black olives, and anchovy is meant to be consumed soon after its elements have had an opportunity to set and congeal. Chef Didier Oudill suggests using jarred belly tuna imported from Italy and Spain, but you can use your favorite brand of canned white tuna in oil.

1. A day or two before: Preheat the oven to 425°F. Cut the eggplant in half lengthwise, place skin side down in a baking pan, sprinkle with the sugar, thyme, salt, and pepper, drizzle with 3 tablespoons olive oil, and roast until very tender, about 35 minutes. Remove from the oven and let cool.

2. Scoop out the flesh from the eggplant into a food processor, add the garlic and cooking juices from the pan, and process until pureed.

3. Combine the tomatoes, roasted peppers, anchovies, and basil in a bowl, drizzle with vinegar and 2 tablespoons olive oil, season with salt and pepper, and mix well.

4. Place the pureed eggplant on the bottom of two small (8 to 10 ounce) Mason or jam jars, top each with a little of the tuna, then the tomato mixture, the remainder of the tuna, and the olives. Seal the jars and refrigerate for at least 24 hours and up to 3 days.

5. To serve, lightly season the arugula leaves with a little olive oil, salt, and pepper. Open the jars and stick the stems of the arugula leaves into the tuna mixture. Serve cold with toast.

CURED SALMON *with* BOILED NEW POTATOES

◦ SAUMON MARINÉ FAÇON HARENG ◦

MAKES 6 TO 8 SERVINGS

3 tablespoons sugar

3 tablespoons salt

2 pounds skinless salmon
   fillets, cut into strips or
   pieces 1/3 to 1/2 inch thick

1 cup red wine vinegar

2 tablespoons olive oil

1 tablespoon vegetable oil

2 stems fresh thyme

2 stems fresh rosemary

2 bay leaves

2 teaspoons black
   peppercorns

1 tablespoon coriander seeds

3 red onions, thinly sliced

4 carrots, thinly sliced,
   peeled

2 pounds new or red skin
   potatoes

Chef Rodolphe Paquin chose to rethink the bistro classic of marinated herrings and boiled potatoes by replacing the smoked herrings with salmon fillets. With several colleagues following his example, you're now just as likely to encounter the salmon version of the dish at better bistros as you are the herring original. Cooked in its marinade, like a seviche, the salmon fillets absorb the flavor of fresh herbs along with the refreshing pungency of onions, vinegar, and coriander seeds.

1. At least 2 days before serving: Combine the sugar and salt and rub this mixture on the salmon strips to coat both sides. Place the strips in flat layers in a glass bowl, ceramic dish, or plastic container, cover with plastic wrap, and let marinate in the refrigerator for 24 hours.

2. Rinse and thoroughly dry all the salmon strips. Combine the vinegar, olive oil, and vegetable oil in a bowl and mix well. Stir in the thyme, rosemary, bay leaves, peppercorns, and coriander seeds to complete the marinade.

3. Layer half the onions on the bottom of a glass bowl or deep ceramic dish suitable for serving. Top with the salmon strips and the remaining onions and carrots and cover all with the marinade. Cover with plastic wrap and refrigerate for at least 24 hours and up to 4 days. Remove the bay leaves.

4. About 45 minutes before serving, scrub the potatoes, place in a saucepan, cover with cold salted water, heat to a boil, and simmer until tender, about 25 minutes. Drain and set aside just until cool enough to handle. Peel, cut into thick slices, and serve warm with the cured salmon and garnishes in their marinade.

SALMON TERRINE *with* LEEKS *and* PESTO

◦ PRESSÉ DE SAUMON AU PISTOU ◦

MAKES 8 TO 10 SERVINGS

11 tablespoons extra virgin olive oil

6 garlic cloves, crushed, and 2 garlic cloves

2 onions, chopped

2 carrots, peeled and sliced

1 cup dry white wine

6 sprigs fresh flat-leaf parsley

2 sprigs thyme

2 bay leaves

Salt

Freshly ground black pepper

6 leeks

1½ cups fresh basil leaves

½ cup pine nuts

½ cup freshly grated Parmigiano-Reggiano

2 pounds salmon fillets, cut into thin slices

1 envelope (2 teaspoons) unflavored gelatin powder

Coarse sea salt

Although chef Sylvain Danière usually prepares this terrine at his bistro with skate wing, his splendid salmon version is less complicated to prepare and more colorful to behold. The result, once sliced, is a beautiful mosaic of pink, red, and several shades of green.

1. Heat 3 tablespoons olive oil in a stockpot over medium heat, add 4 crushed garlic cloves, the onions, and carrots, and cook, stirring occasionally and not letting the vegetables brown, for 5 minutes. Pour the wine into the pot, increase the heat to high, and cook until the liquid is reduced by two-thirds, 3 to 5 minutes. Add 2 quarts cold water, the parsley, thyme, and bay leaves, season with salt and pepper, and heat to a boil. Skim off the foam that has risen to the top, remove from the heat, cover, and set aside for 20 minutes.

2. Trim the base of the leeks and then trim off enough of their green tops so that the leeks are the same length as a 4 to 5-cup terrine pan or loaf pan. Tie the leeks with string in two places and simmer in gently boiling salted water until tender, 13 to 15 minutes. Carefully remove the leeks from the pot, pat them dry with paper towels, and let cool. Cut off the string from the leeks, make a ¼-inch slit down the length of each leek, and peel off the outer leaves, leaving a center core roughly the diameter of a pencil. If some or all of the cores are larger than that, halve those lengthwise. Reserve both the leaves and inner cores.

3. Prepare the pesto: Place the basil leaves and the crushed garlic in a food processor or blender and process until the leaves and garlic cloves are finely chopped. Add the pine nuts and process until finely chopped. Add the cheese and process until fully incorporated. With the motor running, add 5 to 6 tablespoons olive oil in a thin drizzle. Set aside.

Piment d'Espelette or substitute ancho powder or other medium-hot chili powder

4 to 5 small to medium tomatoes

Thin toasts or bread crisps

4. Return the vegetable stock to the stove and heat to a boil. Remove from the heat, submerge the salmon fillets in the stock, cover, and leave the fillets just until cooked through, 10 to 15 minutes. Carefully remove the fillets from the broth with a slotted spoon or spatula, remove and discard their skins if they have any, and set aside. Strain the broth through a cheesecloth-lined sieve and discard the solids.

5. Sprinkle the gelatin into ¼ cup cold water and let sit until softened, 5 minutes. Pour 1½ cups of the stock into a small saucepan over medium heat and cook until it steams but does not boil. Remove from the heat, stir in the gelatin mixture, and set aside.

6. Rinse the inside of the terrine pan or loaf pan with cold water, leaving its inside surface slightly wet. Line the pan with plastic wrap, leaving enough to overlap the edges by at least 4 inches. Starting with the short sides of the pan, stick a leek leaf into the pan and press it over the bottom of the pan and up the side so that the green part is flattened on the bottom of the pan, the lighter part runs up against the side, and the white part overlaps the pan by a couple of inches. Repeat with the remaining leaves, letting each overlap slightly, until the bottom and sides of the pan are completely covered.

7. Using the largest salmon fillet pieces first, cover the bottom of the leek-lined pan with a third of the fillets. Sprinkle with salt and a little piment d'Espelette and top with half the pesto sauce spread out in a thin layer. Arrange half the leek cores lengthwise (parallel to the pan) in a single layer over the pesto. Press the leek cores down and then pour just enough of the gelatin mixture (⅓ to ½ cup) to fill the gaps between the leek cores and salmon fillets. Top with a second layer of salmon fillets and sprinkle with salt and piment d'Espelette. Top with the remainder of the pesto and the tomatoes, pressing the tomatoes down into the terrine, and pour just enough of the gelatin mixture (⅓ to ½ cup) over the tomatoes to fill the gaps. Top with a third layer of salmon fillets and the remainder of the leek cores and press them into the pan. If liquid does not cover the leeks, pour enough of the gelatin mixture over the leeks to cover them and just about fill the pan. Cover the top of the terrine with

the overlapping leek leaves and then the overlapping plastic wrap, pressing it down into the leeks, and refrigerate until set, at least 6 hours and up to 2 days.

8. To serve, unmold the terrine and, leaving the plastic wrap on, carefully cut the terrine into 1-inch slices with a long, very sharp knife. To avoid a collapse of the terrine, do not apply pressure when slicing it. Rely only on the sharp blade of the knife, using it like a saw to slowly cut the terrine. Unwrap the slices and serve them one to a plate with some toasts or crisps. Keep any unserved portion refrigerated.

SESAME FRIED MUSSELS *with* SWEET POTATO PUREE

◦ MOULES EN COQUE DE SÉSAME ET PATATE DOUCE ◦

MAKES 6 APPETIZER
SERVINGS OR 4 MAIN-
COURSE SERVINGS

1 pound sweet potatoes,
  scrubbed clean

Salt

Freshly ground black pepper

3 tablespoons olive oil

1 onion, chopped

1 large carrot, peeled and
  chopped

½ cup dry white wine

2½ pounds mussels,
  scrubbed and debearded

1 cup heavy cream

1 teaspoon curry powder

2 tablespoons unsalted
  butter, cut into small cubes

¼ cup sesame seeds

3 tablespoons bread crumbs

Vegetable oil, for frying

1 egg, beaten

Served alone, the sesame-coated fried mussels are a splendid hors d'oeuvre. Scattering them atop a mound of sweet potato puree promotes them to the status of a great starter, cleverly blurring the distinction between sweet and savory. Encircling the mussels and the puree with a curry cream sauce elevates it to the class of destination dish. Incredibly, François Pasteau introduced the ensemble as an amuse-bouche, a complimentary tidbit offered to diners in a single-spoon serving.

1. Place the unpeeled sweet potatoes in a pot of boiling water and boil until very tender, 45 to 50 minutes. Drain and, once cool enough to handle, split them, scoop out the pulp, season with salt and pepper, mash with a potato masher, and cover to keep warm.

2. Heat the olive oil in a large saucepan over medium heat, add the onion and carrot, and cook, stirring frequently, until the onion is translucent, 6 to 7 minutes. Add the wine and mussels, raise the heat to moderately high, cover, and cook until the shells have opened, 4 to 6 minutes. Lift the mussels from the pot with a slotted spoon, remove the mussels from their shells, and drain on paper towels. Strain the liquid through a fine sieve to remove the solids. Return the broth to the saucepan and heat over moderately high heat until the liquid is reduced by half, 3 to 5 minutes. Add the cream and heat, stirring with a whisk, to a boil. Stir in the curry powder, remove from the heat, and add the butter, piece by piece, beating each into the sauce until dissolved before adding the next piece. Cover and keep warm. (If you need to reheat the sauce, do so over a very low flame so the sauce does not break.)

3. Combine the sesame seeds and bread crumbs and spread the mixture on the bottom of a shallow plate. Clip a deep-frying thermometer to a heavy-bottomed saucepan and heat 2 inches of oil over high heat to a temperature of 350 to 360°F. Dip the mussels in the beaten egg and roll in the sesame seed–bread crumb mixture. Fry quickly, working in batches if necessary, until lightly golden, about 3 minutes, and drain on paper towels.

4. To serve, spoon a mound of sweet potato puree in the center of six plates (four plates if serving as a main course) and flatten each a little with the back of a spoon. Top the sweet potatoes with about 6 fried mussels (8 mussels per main course serving) and pour curry cream sauce around the potatoes.

L'Épi Dupin's François Pasteau trespasses the boundaries between sweet and savory.

SESAME SALMON FINGERS

⊙ GOUJONNETTES DE SAUMON ⊙

MAKES 4 SERVINGS

12 ounces skinless salmon fillets, sliced into ½-inch strips

Salt

½ cup sesame seeds

Peanut oil, for frying, or substitute vegetable oil

1 cup Tartar Sauce (page 29)

Mixed greens or Warm Lentil Salad (page 62)

Vinaigrette (page 47)

This brasserie's unbattered goujonnettes *are delectable as an appetizer or a finger food, especially when served with a classic French tartar sauce.*

1. Sprinkle the salmon strips with salt. Place the sesame seeds on a plate and dip the salmon strips to thoroughly coat on all sides.

2. Clip a deep-frying thermometer to a heavy-bottomed saucepan and heat 2 inches of oil over high heat to 360°F. Fry the fish fingers in batches until the sesame seeds are golden, 2 to 3 minutes. Drain on paper towels. Serve with tartar sauce and either mixed greens drizzled with vinaigrette or lentil salad.

Salt Cod *and* Avocado Brandade *with* Fresh Cilantro

◦ BRANDADE DE MORUE ET AVOCAT À LA CORIANDRE FRAÎCHE ◦

MAKES 6 APPETIZER
SERVINGS

1 pound salt cod fillets

2 bay leaves

3 sprigs fresh thyme

1 cup milk

3 ripe avocados (preferably
Hass), peeled and pitted

4 tablespoons freshly
squeezed lime juice

2 teaspoons lime zest

2 plum tomatoes, seeded
and finely chopped

1 small red onion, finely
chopped

1/2 cup chopped fresh
cilantro

1 1/2 teaspoons coarse sea
salt

Freshly ground black pepper

1/2 to 1 teaspoon piment
d'Espelette or ancho
powder or other medium-
hot chili powder, optional

French country bread, sliced
and toasted, or substitute
tortilla chips

Workable as an appetizer, party snack, side dish, picnic treat, or summer main course, this guacamole-like puree is named after Provence's brandade de morue *and largely inspired by the French Carribean's* féroce d'avocat. *The former is a puree of salt cod, milk, olive oil, and garlic; the latter, a peppery blend of avocado, manioc flour, and either crab or cod. Though this recipe calls for a smooth puree whipped up in a food processor, you may prefer a lumpier version mashed by hand in a bowl or—why not?—a Mexican* molcajete.

1. The day before you plan to serve: Soak the salt cod fillets in cold water, changing the water 3 or 4 times, for 24 hours. Drain.

2. Combine the bay leaves, thyme, milk, and 3 cups water in a large saucepan and heat over moderately high heat to a simmer. Add the salt cod fillets, lower the heat to low, and cook at a gentle simmer (do not boil, or the salt cod will harden) until the salt cod flakes easily when tested with a fork, 10 to 15 minutes. Drain in a colander, discard the bay leaves, remove any remaining bones, pat dry with paper towels, and flake the cod with a fork into small pieces.

3. Combine the salt cod, 2 avocados, the lime juice, and lime zest in a food processor and process until smooth. Transfer to a large bowl, add the tomatoes, red onion, cilantro, and salt and season with pepper and, if desired, piment d'Espelette or other chili powder. Dice the remaining avocado, add it to the bowl, and mix well. Correct the seasoning and serve with toast or tortilla chips.

WARM LENTIL SALAD

◦ SALADE DE LENTILLES ◦

MAKES 4 SERVINGS

1 cup French green lentils

1 small onion

2 whole cloves

1 garlic clove

1 small carrot, peeled and
   quartered lengthwise

1 bay leaf

1 shallot, minced

2 tablespoons chopped
   parsley

3 tablespoons extra virgin
   olive oil

1 tablespoon sherry vinegar

Salt

Freshly ground black pepper

The key to this and other recipes for French lentil salad is the use of French green lentils from Puy, partly because their slightly sweet taste and delicately crisp texture may be the finest in the world but also because they come from the volcanic plateaus surrounding the town of Le Puy en Velay in Auvergne, the region also known for cultivating leaders in the bistro and brasserie trades. Although Wepler, like many brasseries, is Alsatian in name and origin, it has been run since 1976 by the Bessière family, which hails from Aveyron, just down the N88 motorway from the land of the Puy lentils. To retain the crisp texture for which they are prized, do not cook the Puy lentils for more than 25 minutes.

1. Wash and drain the lentils, place them in a saucepan, cover with 2 inches of cold water, and heat to a boil.

2. Stud the onion with the cloves and add it, the garlic, carrot, and bay leaf to the lentils. Cover, lower the heat to very low, and simmer until the moisture has been absorbed, about 25 minutes. Remove from the heat, remove and discard the onion, garlic, carrot, and bay leaf. Transfer to a large bowl, add the shallot and parsley, and mix well.

3. Combine the olive oil and sherry vinegar in a small bowl and beat well with a whisk. Pour this vinaigrette over the lentils, season with salt and pepper, and toss well. Serve warm or at room temperature.

MACKEREL CROQUETTES

◦ CROQUETTES DE MACQUEREAU ◦

MAKES 6 SERVINGS

1 bottle white wine

3 shallots, coarsely chopped

3 to 4 sprigs thyme

1 bay leaf

1 lemon, washed and halved

Salt

Freshly ground black pepper

1¼ pounds mackerel fillets

1¼ pounds Yukon gold or
   Idaho russet potatoes,
   peeled

3 tablespoons unsalted
   butter, softened, at room
   temperature

Pinch of nutmeg

Pinch of piment d'Espelette
   or ancho powder or other
   medium-hot chili powder,
   optional

2 eggs, beaten

1 cup bread crumbs

Oil, for frying

Tartar Sauce (page 29)

There is a growing movement within the bistro community to enhance the image of the maligned mackerel, a moist, oily, richly flavored, and, yes, inexpensive fish with a stinky reputation. Clémentine prepares its mackerel in the safest and most comforting of formats, the fish croquette. Serve the croquettes with vinaigrette-drizzled mixed greens.

1. Prepare a simplified court-bouillon: Combine the wine, shallots, thyme, bay leaf, lemon halves, and 1 quart cold water in a saucepan, season with salt and pepper, and bring to a boil. Lower the heat and simmer for 30 minutes. Strain out the solid ingredients and bring the strained liquid back to a boil. Remove from the heat, add the mackerel fillets, cover, and leave until the fillets are cooked through, about 10 minutes. Remove the mackerel from the liquid, drain, and flake thoroughly with a fork.

2. Cut the potatoes into 1-inch cubes, and cook in boiling salted water until tender, about 15 minutes. Drain well and pass through a potato ricer or mash with a potato masher. Place in a large mixing bowl, add the butter in small amounts, and mix until incorporated.

3. Add the mackerel to the potatoes, season with nutmeg and, if desired, piment d'Espelette, and mix thoroughly with a spatula until the mixture is homogeneous, about 5 minutes. Roll the mixture into balls about 2 to 2½ inches in diameter. Combine the beaten eggs and 2 tablespoons cold water in a small bowl. Dip the fish balls in the beaten eggs, letting the excess egg drip back into the bowl, and roll in the bread crumbs.

4. Clip a deep-frying thermometer to a heavy-bottomed saucepan and heat 3 inches of oil over high heat to 350°F. Fry the fish croquettes in small batches until golden brown, 3 to 4 minutes. Drain on paper towels and serve with tartar sauce.

WARM SALAD OF RED MULLETS *with* SHREDDED BEETS *and* BASIL SAUCE

◦ SALADE TIÈDE DE ROUGET AUX BETTERAVES RÂPÉES ET JUS DE BASILIC ◦

MAKES 4 SERVINGS

2 pounds beets

1 garlic clove, chopped

3 tablespoons red wine vinegar

½ cup extra virgin olive oil

Salt

Freshly ground black pepper

2 cups loosely packed basil leaves

4 red mullet fillets or substitute red snapper fillets, about 4 ounces each

The Mediterranean rouget, *also called* rouget barbet, *varies in length from 5 to 15 inches. The smaller ones are served whole; the larger specimens, as fillets. Seldom is their preparation very complicated. Though they are often grilled, chef Thierry Faucher prefers to drizzle them with olive oil and quickly bake them. This wine bar salad is basic and beautiful, the beets and basil providing brilliant color and two very different notions of sweetness to the ensemble.*

1. Preheat the oven to 400°F. Peel, rinse, pat dry, and shred the beets using either a food processor or the large holes of a grater. Combine the garlic, vinegar, and 2 tablespoons olive oil and pour over the shredded beets. Season with salt and pepper, toss well, and refrigerate for at least 1 hour.

2. Place the basil leaves and ¼ teaspoon salt in a food processor and process until finely chopped. With the motor running, slowly add 2 tablespoons olive oil and process until fully incorporated. Stir in ½ cup boiling water and set aside.

3. Wash and pat dry the mullet fillets, place them in a baking dish, drizzle on both sides with olive oil, season on both sides with salt and pepper, and bake just until cooked through or when the fish flakes easily, 10 to 15 minutes.

4. To serve, place a mound of shredded beets on four plates, top with the fillets, and drizzle the entire plate with basil sauce.

SEARED SCALLOPS *with* CELERY ROOT *and* GREEN APPLE RÉMOULADE

◦ NOIX DE SAINT JACQUES RÔTIES, RÉMOULADE DE CÉLERI AUX POMMES VERTES ◦

MAKES 4 SERVINGS

One 1-pound celery root

1½ tablespoons fresh lemon juice

1 Granny Smith apple, peeled, cored, and diced

⅔ cup Classic Mayonnaise (page 31)

2 teaspoons Dijon mustard

2 tablespoons chopped chives

4 tablespoons extra virgin olive oil

1 tablespoon balsamic vinegar

Salt

Freshly ground black pepper

12 sea scallops

Many bistros pair scallops with Belgian endive, its slightly bitter flavor a natural complement to the mild sweetness of the sea scallops. Chef Bruno Doucet breaks up this prevalent pairing, substituting the gentle pungency and mild sweetness of raw celery root and the tartness of the Granny Smith apple for the endive.

1. Peel the brown outside off the celery root and shred using either a food processor or the large holes of a grater. Immediately combine in a bowl with the lemon juice and toss to prevent yellowing of the celery root.

2. Add the apple, mayonnaise, mustard, and chives, mix well, and set aside.

3. Prepare a vinaigrette: Combine 3 tablespoons olive oil and the balsamic vinegar, season with salt and pepper, and beat with a whisk. Set aside.

4. Heat the remaining 1 tablespoon olive oil in a nonstick skillet over high heat. Sear the scallops until lightly browned, about 30 seconds on each side.

5. To serve, place a mound of celery root and apple rémoulade in the center of four plates, surround each with 4 scallops, and drizzle a little vinaigrette over the scallops and around the rim of the plate.

SALAD OF BREADED PIG'S FEET

○ SALADE DE CROUSTILLANTS DE PIEDS DE COCHON ○

MAKES 6 SERVINGS

6 ounces haricots verts or slender green beans, trimmed

6 cups mesclun greens

2 fresh pig's feet

1 celery stick, cut into chunks

¾ cup white wine vinegar

Salt

Freshly ground black pepper

2 whole eggs

½ cup bread crumbs

½ cup ground almonds

½ cup vegetable oil, plus 3 tablespoons for the vinaigrette

3 tablespoons balsamic vinegar

2 tablespoons hazelnut oil

2 tablespoons chopped toasted hazelnuts

This salad, with its golden rounds of breaded pig's feet, serves as an appealing introduction to pied de cochon, *a specialty from which this famous brasserie takes its name. But you could easily dispose of the greens and serve the crisp, nutty rounds with* frites *and béarnaise sauce. Fresh pig's feet (also called trotters) are sold, usually for a pittance, at many Italian, Chinese, Latin American, or other ethnic butchers.*

1. Cook the haricots verts in boiling salted water until crisp-tender, 3 to 4 minutes. Drain, plunge into ice water, drain again, and pat dry. Combine with the mesclun greens in a large bowl.

2. Rinse the pig's feet thoroughly in cold water for several minutes and drain. Wrap each with several strips of cheesecloth or tie tightly and thoroughly with string. Place in a pot with the celery, vinegar, salt, pepper, and enough water to cover by 3 inches and heat to a boil. Lower the heat to very low and simmer gently for 5 hours. Remove from the heat and let cool in the broth.

3. Remove the cheesecloth, cut each pig's foot in half, remove the bones, roll each section tightly in plastic wrap, and refrigerate until firm.

4. Place the eggs in a bowl, season with salt and pepper, and beat well. Mix together the bread crumbs and ground almonds in a separate plate. Remove the plastic from the pig's feet and cut them into 1-inch-thick rounds. Dip the rounds into the eggs, letting the excess drip back into the bowl, and then roll in the bread crumbs to coat the pig's feet completely on both sides.

5. Heat ½ cup vegetable oil in a skillet over moderately high heat and fry the breaded rounds until crisp and golden, about 3 minutes per side. Drain on paper towels.

6. Combine the vinegar, hazelnut oil, and 3 tablespoons vegetable oil and beat with a whisk. Pour over the mesclun greens and haricots verts, season with salt and pepper, and toss.

7. To serve, place the greens in the center of six plates, surround with 3 or 4 rounds of pig's feet, and scatter the hazelnuts over the greens.

Directeur *Jean-François Lecerf, a fixture at Au Pied de Cochon since 1964.*

Soups

✳

SOUPES

GARLIC SOUP *with* MUSSELS

◦ TOURIN À L'AIL AUX MOULES ◦

MAKES 4 SERVINGS

2 pounds mussels, scrubbed
  and bearded

1 cup dry white wine

3 tablespoons olive oil

6 garlic cloves, minced

1 baguette, cut into
  ½-inch slices

1 egg yolk

1 tablespoon red wine
  vinegar

1 cup (4 ounces) grated
  Gruyère

1 to 2 teaspoons piment
  d'Espelette or substitute
  ancho powder or other
  medium-hot chili powder

The Tourin à l'Ail *Gérard Fouché prepares for his Parisian clientele at Le Bistrot des Capucins differs from the rustic garlic soup of his Bordeaux boyhood in two significant ways: He adds mussels to the milky white broth and removes the often bitter green germ in the center of the garlic cloves used to prepare it. His mother, a native of the Dordogne region of southwestern France, would never contemplate trimming her garlic.*

"In the south," notes Fouché, "when someone says bonjour *and you don't smell the garlic, you say, 'What's the matter? Why didn't you eat lunch today?'"*

He suggests stretching the soup into a meal with the addition of vermicelli, which would cook in the simmering mussel broth. With or without noodles, the soup is savored to the very last drop through a custom known as faire charbot: *A little red wine is poured into the empty soup bowl to absorb the last traces of the* tourin, *which in turn is sopped up with any remaining scraps of a baguette.*

1. Place the mussels, wine, and 1 cup cold water in a large saucepan over moderately high heat, cover, and cook until the shells open up, 4 to 6 minutes. Strain the mussels into a colander, collecting the juices in a bowl placed below.

2. Heat the olive oil in a saucepan over low heat, add the garlic, and cook, stirring constantly, until pale gold, 3 to 4 minutes (do not let the garlic brown).

3. Add the mussel juice to the garlic, raise the heat to medium, and bring to a boil. Cover, lower the heat to very low, and simmer for 10 minutes.

4. Meanwhile, remove the mussels from the shells. Lightly toast most of the bread slices.

5. Remove the soup from the heat. Combine the egg yolk, vinegar, and a couple of tablespoons of the soup in a mixing bowl and beat vigorously with a whisk until the mixture gets foamy. Slowly pour this mixture back into the remaining soup, continuing to beat with a whisk.

6. To serve, place a few baguette slices, 3 or 4 tablespoons of grated cheese, and some mussels on the bottom of four wide soup bowls, cover with soup, and dust with piment d'Espelette.

CREAM OF MUSHROOM SOUP

○ CRÈME DE CHAMPIGNONS ○

MAKES 6 SERVINGS

6 tablespoons unsalted butter

2 onions, finely chopped

1 garlic clove, crushed

1 pound white button mushrooms, chopped

5 cups chicken broth

1 bay leaf

3 to 4 sprigs thyme

Salt

Freshly ground black pepper

1/4 pound fresh wild mushrooms (one variety), cleaned, trimmed, and chopped, such as chanterelles or shiitakes

2 cups heavy cream

1/4 cup pine nuts

Garlic Croutons (recipe follows)

Thierry Faucher has neither the time nor the inclination to complicate his classic cream of mushroom soup. For lunches and dinners at La Cave, the wine bar he can see from the kitchen window of his bistro (l'Os à Moelle), he wants things that are quick, true to flavor, and efficient. As such, flourishes and garnitures depend on what's lying around. If he's serving sautéed foie gras in his bistro he might sauté some chopped wild mushrooms in the fat rendered by the foie gras. If he has chicken breast left from another recipe, he'll add strips of it to the soup. Or, if it's asparagus season, he might boil some up and add it to the soup.

1. Heat 4 tablespoons butter in a saucepan over medium heat, add the onions and garlic and cook, stirring frequently, for 3 minutes. Add the white button mushrooms and cook, stirring occasionally, until they are tender, about 12 minutes.

2. Pour the chicken broth over the mushrooms. Tie the bay leaf and thyme together with kitchen twine and add to the soup, season with salt and pepper, and heat to a boil. Lower the heat and simmer for 30 minutes.

3. Heat the remaining 2 tablespoons butter in a skillet over medium heat, add the chopped wild mushrooms, season with salt and pepper, and cook, stirring occasionally, just until tender, about 8 minutes. Remove from the heat and set aside.

4. Remove the soup from the heat, remove the tied herbs, pour the soup into a food processor or blender, and process until smooth. Pass the soup through a fine sieve back into the saucepan and re-heat, whisking in the cream. Correct the seasoning.

5. To serve, place some of the sautéed mushrooms, pine nuts, and garlic croutons on the bottom of six soup bowls and ladle the soup over them.

GARLIC CROUTONS
(croutons à l'ail)

MAKES 6 TO 8 SERVINGS

3 tablespoons unsalted butter or extra virgin olive oil

2 garlic cloves, chopped

2 cups tiny bread cubes, cut from day-old baguette or other crusty bread

French croutons are generally either larger or smaller than American salad croutons. The large ones are essentially round or oval toasts, the French counterpart to Italian crostini. The tiny ones represented in this recipe are usually no bigger than a ¼-inch square and add gritty crunch to soups, salads, or omelets. For crostini-like croutons, simply fry thin rounds of a baguette in garlic and butter or oil.

Melt the butter in a saucepan over medium heat, add the garlic, and cook for 3 minutes, not letting the garlic brown. Add the bread cubes and cook, tossing them frequently with the garlic, until brown on all sides, about 3 minutes. Drain on paper towels and let cool.

Thierry Faucher, chef-owner of La Cave à l'Os à Moelle and its parent bistro.

ONION SOUP GRATINÉE

◦ SOUPE À L'OIGNON GRATINÉE "TRADITION" ◦

MAKES 6 SERVINGS

4 tablespoons unsalted
 butter

1½ pounds onions, minced

2 cups dry white wine

2 quarts beef stock

Bouquet garni (1 bay leaf, 1
 sprig fresh thyme, 3 sprigs
 fresh parsley)

Salt

Freshly ground black pepper

½ pound Emmentaler or
 Gruyère

1 baguette, thinly sliced and
 lightly toasted

The bulldozing in 1970 of Les Halles, Paris's main wholesale food market, amounted to a kick in the gut—Zola called Les Halles "the belly of Paris"—from which the city has never fully recovered. There is, however, one consistent source of consolation: The brasserie that diligently fed the white-aproned workers of Les Halles for over forty years still serves an exemplary, round-the-clock onion soup gratinée. In the unsettling flux of daily life, the very existence of a 24/7 gratinée in the heart, if no longer the stomach, of the French capital is a source of great comfort even to those with no sentimental attachment to the old market and its massive iron-and-glass pavilions. Like a dear friend, Au Pied de Cochon's gratinée is there for you when you need it most, day or night. You don't even have to call.

The superiority of Au Pied de Cochon's onion soup gratinée owes as much to its execution as to its recipe. With an average of fifty requests for it every day, winter and summer alike, it's both a priority and a preoccupation. To ensure a deep, rich, but not excessively sweet soup, take care that the onions cook slowly to a deep golden color. Check on the cheese in the broiler so that it melts and bubbles but does not blister. If you plan on preparing the soup in advance, stop at the conclusion of step 1, let the soup cool, refrigerate in a covered container for up to 24 hours, and reheat it slowly over a low flame before proceeding to step 2. For a soup nearly light enough to qualify as an appetizer, substitute a quart of water for a quart of beef stock or replace the beef stock with a quart each of chicken stock and water.

1. Melt the butter in a large stockpot over medium heat, add the onions, and cook, stirring frequently, until the onions are soft and a rich, uniformly golden-caramel color sets in (but do not brown), 25 to 30 minutes. Add the wine, raise the heat to high, and boil until the liquid is reduced by half, about 15 minutes. Add the beef stock

and bouquet garni and bring just to a boil. Reduce the heat to low, and cook at a gentle simmer for 1 hour. Remove the bouquet garni from the soup and correct the seasoning. (If your stock is well seasoned you won't need much, if any, salt and pepper.)

2. Preheat the broiler. Grate the cheese using the large holes of a box grater. Place one or two slices of toasted baguette on the bottom of six ovenproof soup bowls. Ladle the soup into the bowls and sprinkle liberally with a thick layer of grated cheese. Set the bowls in the broiler, 4 inches from the flame, until the cheese turns bubbly and golden but not too brown, 3 to 4 minutes. Serve immediately.

Chef Elvis Carcel applies the finishing touches to the first of fifty daily gratinées.

FISH IN BROTH

◦ POISSON ET SA SOUPE ◦

MAKES 4 SERVINGS

4 whole red mullets, 8 to 10
  ounces each or substitute
  2 pounds red snapper,
  smallest size available

3 tablespoons olive oil

2 teaspoons chopped fresh
  thyme

1 large garlic clove, crushed

2 tablespoons tomato paste

1/2 cup dry white wine

Salt

Piment d'Espelette or chili
  powder

Garlic Croutons (page 73)

In this most basic of bistro fish soups, the fish heads and bones flavor a broth that in turn flavors the fillets in their final cooking phase. It is not imperative that you pass the soup through a food mill, though it is an effective way to extract their juices. You may skip that step by pressing down on the bones and heads in a fine strainer so that most of their juices pass through. Prepare the croutons as thin rounds rather than tiny cubes.

1. Scale, gut, wash, and fillet the red mullets or ask your fishmonger to do this, being sure to keep the center bones and head. Pat the fillets dry, place them in a baking dish, drizzle with 1 tablespoon olive oil, sprinkle with the thyme, cover with plastic wrap, and refrigerate for at least 1 hour.

2. Preheat the oven to 400°F. Heat the remaining 2 tablespoons olive oil in a saucepan over moderately high heat. Add the garlic and cook, stirring occasionally, for 2 to 3 minutes, being careful not to let it brown. Add the fish bones and heads and cook, stirring once or twice, for 2 minutes. Add the tomato paste and cook for an additional 1 minute. Add the wine and cook until the liquid is reduced by half, about 3 minutes. Add 3 cups water and bring to a boil. Lower the heat and simmer for 15 to 20 minutes.

3. Pass the soup, bones, and heads through a food mill to squeeze out every last drop of juice. Pass the soup through a strainer to remove any remaining bones and season the strained fish soup to taste with salt and piment d'Espelette. Return to the saucepan and heat, covered, over low heat until ready to serve.

4. Remove the plastic wrap covering the fillets and bake them until not quite cooked through, 5 to 8 minutes. (They will finish cooking in the broth.)

5. To serve, place 2 fillets and 2 or 3 croutons on the bottom of four shallow bowls. Ladle enough soup into the bowl to cover the fillets. Keep the remaining soup warm and refill bowls as needed.

Mackerel Soup: Substitute mackerel (about 3 pounds) for the red mullets and chopped fresh cilantro for the thyme. Larger mackerel fillets will have to cook longer, 8 to 15 minutes, depending on size.

Sardine Soup: Substitute 12 to 16 whole sardines for the red mullets, 1 teaspoon hazelnut oil for 1 teaspoon (a third) of the olive oil used to marinate the fillets, and chopped fresh chervil or parsley for the thyme.

ENDIVE CURRY SOUP *with* CARROTS *and* MUSSELS

◦ VELOUTÉ D'ENDIVES AU COLUMBO, PETITS LÉGUMES AUX MOULES ◦

MAKES 6 SERVINGS

2 pounds Belgian endive

½ cup plus 2 tablespoons olive oil

1 to 2 tablespoons colombo powder or curry powder

1 tablespoon sugar

1½ quarts chicken stock

2 tablespoons fresh lemon juice

Salt

Freshly ground black pepper

½ to 1 teaspoon piment d'Espelette or ancho powder or other medium-hot chili powder, optional

2 pounds mussels, cleaned and debearded

½ pound carrots, peeled and finely chopped

2 medium red onions, finely chopped

1 bunch chives, finely chopped

The seasoning of this contemporary bistro's soup depends on the bitterness of the Belgian endive and the potency of the colombo powder. Colombo is a curry-like blend of spices brought to the French West Indies by migrant laborers from Sri Lanka. Don't add additional colombo if it's a hot, spicier zip you're after. Better to sprinkle in some piment d'Espelette or cayenne. The balance between bitterness and sweetness can be controlled with the addition of lemon juice or sugar.

1. Trim the bottom third of the endive and cut away any browned areas. Finely chop the leaves.

2. Heat 3 tablespoons olive oil over medium heat, add the endive, and cook, stirring frequently, until soft and translucent but not colored, about 5 minutes. Add the colombo powder, sugar, chicken stock, and lemon juice, season with salt, pepper, and, if desired, piment d'Espelette, and heat to just under a boil. Cover, lower the heat to low, and simmer for 30 minutes.

3. Place the mussels in a pot with 1 to 2 inches boiling water, cover, and steam over high heat until the shells open, 6 to 9 minutes. Drain the mussels and once they are cool enough to handle remove them from their shells and set aside.

4. Taste the soup and adjust the seasoning: If it's too sour, add a little more sugar and a few drops of lemon juice. Then stir in ⅓ cup olive oil, cover, and keep warm over very low heat.

5. Heat 2 tablespoons olive oil in a saucepan over medium heat, add the carrots and onions and cook, stirring occasionally, until the onions are translucent but not browned, 7 to 9 minutes. Add the mussels and cook, stirring once or twice, for 1 minute. Correct the seasoning. Pour the mixture through a fine strainer to drain out the liquid.

6. To serve, spoon the vegetable-mussel mixture into soup bowls, ladle the hot endive curry soup on top, and sprinkle with chives.

CREAM OF CARROT SOUP *with* CUMIN

◦ CRÈME DE CAROTTES AU CUMIN ◦

MAKES 4 SERVINGS

3 tablespoons olive oil

2 pounds carrots, peeled and
   cut into 1-inch chunks

2 garlic cloves, crushed

1 teaspoon ground cumin

½ cup freshly squeezed
   orange juice

½ cup heavy cream

Salt

Garlic Croutons (page 73)

Chef-owner Thierry Blanqui transports the classic combination of carrots and cumin from Morocco to his 15th arrondissement bistro in this silkily mellow but hardly bland soup. The tart sweetness of freshly squeezed jus d'orange invigorates the pairing by drawing out the naturally sweet flavor of the carrots so that it stands up to the strong aroma and bitter edge of the cumin.

1. Heat the olive oil in a large saucepan over medium heat. Add the carrots and cook, stirring occasionally, for 5 minutes. Add the garlic and cumin and cook, stirring occasionally and not letting the carrots and garlic color, for 3 minutes.

2. Add the orange juice and 1 quart cold water, raise the heat to high, and heat to a boil. Lower the heat to low and cook at a simmer, uncovered, for 45 minutes, adding a little water from time to time as needed.

3. Transfer to a blender or food processor and puree until completely smooth.

4. Return the soup to the saucepan and set over medium heat. Stir in the cream and cook over medium heat, beating with a whisk, until smooth and slightly thickened, about 2 minutes. Season to taste with salt.

5. To serve, place some garlic croutons on the bottom of four soup bowls and ladle the soup over them.

CHILLED PEA SOUP

⚬ SOUPE GLACÉE AUX PETITS POIS ⚬

MAKES 4 SERVINGS

2 pounds fresh peas

1 quart light cream

2 teaspoons chopped fresh thyme

Salt

Freshly ground black pepper

Garlic Croutons (page 73)

2 thin slices smoked ham, diced

Piment d'Espelette, optional

Thierry Faucher serves his pea soup chilled at his wine bar in summer. He advises against overcooking the peas, which deprives them of their bright color and flavor and light crispness. This is especially important in this chilled pea soup because the peas are left whole; only their shells are pureed.

1. Remove the peas from their shells and reserve the shells. Cook the peas in boiling salted water just until tender, about 6 minutes. Drain, plunge into cold water to stop the cooking process, drain again, and refrigerate.

2. Cook the pea shells in a separate pot of boiling water until tender, 12 to 15 minutes. Drain the shells, combine them with the cream and thyme in a blender or food processor, season with salt and pepper, and puree until smooth. Pass the mixture through a fine strainer and refrigerate.

3. To serve, place a tablespoon or two of croutons, some diced ham, and up to a quarter (about ½ cup) of the peas on the bottom of four soup bowls and ladle the cream soup on top. Dust the top of the soup, if some peppery spice is desired, with a little piment d'Espelette.

Main Courses

PLATS

POACHED SKATE WING *with* BROWN BUTTER SAUCE

◦ RAIE AU BEURRE NOISETTE ◦

MAKES 4 SERVINGS

2 medium skate wings or
   1½ pounds skate wing
   fillets

½ cup red wine vinegar

1 bay leaf

2 sprigs thyme

2 tablespoons coarse sea salt

5 tablespoons unsalted
   butter

Salt

Freshly ground black pepper

3 tablespoons capers,
   drained

¼ cup finely chopped flat-
   leaf parsley

Chef Christian René's preference for skate française *(also described
as* bouclée, "curled") *over skate* américaine *has nothing to do, he
assures us, with national loyalties. The American variety, which he
happily uses when the other is not available, is slightly drier. Dryness
does not, however, appear to be a factor when the skate wing is first
gently poached to prevent its meat from breaking up and then
liberally topped with a silky brown butter sauce. There are many
extremely creative and appealing things being done with skate fish
today, especially with Asian accents, but few if any can match this
classic French version for pure delight.*

1. Wash the skate wings in cold water. Combine in a pot with the
vinegar, bay leaf, thyme, and coarse sea salt, cover with 2 quarts cold
water, and heat over high heat to a rapid boil. Remove the pot from
the heat, cover, and let the skate continue to poach in the hot water
until just cooked through, about 10 minutes.

2. Meanwhile, melt the butter in a saucepan over low heat and continue to cook, stirring constantly with a wooden spoon, until the
butter turns a light brown color and emits a hazelnut-like smell, 8 to
10 minutes. (Do not let the butter blacken.) Remove from the heat
and set aside for another minute, during which time the butter will
continue cooking to a deeper shade of brown. Season with salt and
pepper.

3. Drain the skate wings, peel off the skin with a knife, and cut each
wing in half to create four half-wing portions. Place each on a warm
plate, sprinkle with capers and chopped parsley, and top with brown
butter sauce.

GRILLED TUNA *with* TOMATO MANGO PINEAPPLE SALSA

◦ THON GRILLÉ À GARNITURE ÉTONNANTE ◦

MAKES 6 SERVINGS

⅓ cup freshly squeezed lemon juice

3 tablespoons olive oil

6 tuna steaks (6 to 7 ounces each), about 1 inch thick

Salt

Freshly ground black pepper

1 small red onion, thinly sliced

6 ripe plum tomatoes, chopped

1 mango, diced

1 cup diced pineapple

1 teaspoon chopped fresh ginger

2 tablespoons freshly squeezed lime juice

¼ to ½ teaspoon piment d'Espelette or substitute ancho powder or other medium-hot chili powder

Vegetable oil, for grilling

The actual title of this extremely popular dish, Grilled Tuna with Astonishing Garnish, may seem odd to Americans already accustomed to tomato, mango, and/or pineapple salsa with their seafood. For the French, the preparation is more exotic. What makes the recipe extraordinary for a wine bar like Willi's is that it goes with every wine: white, red, pink, oaky, acidic, fruity, robust, herbaceous, fleshy, earthy, bubbly, whatever. So if your guests are bringing the wine and you don't know what they've chosen, you might as well astonish them, too.

1. Combine the lemon juice and olive oil on a large plate. Sprinkle the tuna steaks with salt and pepper, place them on the plate to coat on both sides, and let marinate for 30 minutes to 1 hour.

2. Separate the onion slices into rings. Place them in a large bowl with the tomatoes, mango, pineapple, ginger, and lime juice. Season to taste with piment d'Espelette, salt, and pepper, and mix well. Set aside.

3. Prepare a medium-hot charcoal fire in a grill, preheat a gas grill, or heat a lightly oiled grill pan over moderately high heat until hot but not smoking. Brush the grill with oil. Remove the tuna steaks from the marinade, place them over the grill, and cook to taste, about 3 minutes on each side for medium. To serve, spoon the salsa over the tuna steaks.

SAUERKRAUT *with* FISH

MAKES 4 SERVINGS

1½ pounds unsweetened sauerkraut (see page 88)

12 tablespoons (1½ sticks) unsalted butter

2 onions, thinly sliced

5 cups dry white wine

2 smoked trout fillets (about 1 pound)

2 teaspoons juniper berries

1 teaspoon black peppercorns

2 bay leaves

4 sprigs fresh thyme

6 shallots, minced

8 small to medium red bliss potatoes

One ½ pound salmon fillet

One ½ pound monkfish fillet

4 large shrimp, unshelled

Freshly ground black pepper

This is a close translation of Bofinger's superlative fish choucroute. The only significant alteration is that it acquires its smokiness from smoked trout instead of smoked haddock (finnan haddie), which is harder to find in North America. Although foreign diners are sometimes attracted to fish choucroute as a low-fat, low-cholesterol alternative to the pork version, Bofinger frustrates such good intentions by generously spooning a beurre blanc *(white butter sauce flavored with wine and shallots) over the bottoms of each plate. This buttery* choucroute de poisson *is nevertheless a good deal lighter than any* choucroute garnie *and therefore the better of the two to serve during the warm-weather months.*

1. Rinse the sauerkraut thoroughly in cold water and squeeze out all the water you can with your hands.

2. Melt 2 tablespoons butter in a large saucepan over medium heat, add the onions, and cook, stirring occasionally, until they're translucent but not colored, 7 to 9 minutes. Add the sauerkraut, cover with 1½ cups wine and 1 cup water, and heat just to a boil.

3. Peel the skin off the trout fillets, cut the ends off the fillets, and wrap the skins and ends in cheesecloth along with the juniper berries, peppercorns, 1 bay leaf, and 2 sprigs fresh thyme. Add this sack to the sauerkraut, lower the heat to low, cover, and simmer for 1½ hours.

4. Prepare a court-bouillon: Melt 2 tablespoons butter in a large saucepan over low heat. Add half the minced shallots and cook for 3 minutes. Cover with 3 cups wine and 3 cups cold water, add 1 bay leaf and the leaves from the remaining thyme sprigs, season with salt, and heat to a boil. Lower the heat to low and simmer for 40 minutes.

5. Cook the potatoes in boiling salted water until soft, about 20 minutes, and then drain.

6. Place the smoked trout fillets in the court-bouillon and simmer until heated through, 2 to 3 minutes. Remove with a slotted spatula or spoon, transfer to a plate, and keep warm in the oven. Simmer the salmon in the same manner until cooked through, about 8 minutes per inch of thickness. Simmer the monkfish fillet until tender, 6 to 8 minutes. Simmer the shrimp just until cooked through, 3 to 4 minutes.

7. Remove the cheesecloth sack from the sauerkraut and season to taste with salt and pepper.

8. Just before serving, prepare a beurre blanc: Combine the remaining minced shallots and ½ cup white wine in a small saucepan and cook over medium heat, stirring constantly, until reduced by half. Pour through a strainer to remove the shallots. Cut 8 tablespoons (1 stick) butter into small cubes. Return the strained liquid to the saucepan, set over low heat, and add the butter, piece by piece, beating continuously with a whisk, until all the butter has melted to form a creamy sauce. Season with salt and pepper.

9. To serve, place the sauerkraut in a large mound in the center of a large serving plate. Prop the shrimp atop the sauerkraut. Cut the fish fillets into smaller pieces, halve the potatoes, and place them around the sauerkraut. Spoon the beurre blanc to cover the bottom of four dinner plates and let the guests serve themselves.

Buying Sauerkraut

The best sauerkraut is bought fresh from barrels. You may be able to find some in the refrigerator section of a local grocer or deli, especially a German or Polish one. Fresh sauerkraut should be refrigerated and used within a week. If fresh is unavailable, try sauerkraut packaged in jars or plastic bags. Avoid canned sauerkraut, which tends to have a flat taste, too much salt, and zero crunch.

SAUERKRAUT *with* SALMON *and* BACON

◦ CHOUCROUTE AU SAUMON ET LARD ◦

MAKES 4 SERVINGS

1½ pounds unsweetened sauerkraut

3 tablespoons unsalted butter

2 onions, minced

2 garlic cloves, chopped

1½ cups dry white wine

2 teaspoons juniper berries

1 teaspoon coriander seeds

2 bay leaves

4 slices slab bacon, each ¼ to ⅓ inch thick

8 small to medium red bliss potatoes

¼ cup white wine vinegar

4 fresh salmon fillets, 5 to 6 ounces each

Freshly ground black pepper

3 to 4 sprigs fresh thyme

Coarse sea salt

In this brasserie's simple and fabulous choucroute, the slab bacon gives some of the smokiness and fattiness of a classic choucroute garnie *to a salmon version.*

1. Rinse the sauerkraut thoroughly in cold water and squeeze out all the water you can with your hands.

2. Melt the butter in a large saucepan over medium heat, add the onions and garlic and cook, stirring occasionally, until the onions are translucent but not colored, 6 to 7 minutes. Add the sauerkraut, cover with the wine and 1 cup water and heat just to a boil.

3. Wrap the juniper berries, coriander seeds, and bay leaves in a cheesecloth, add this sack to the sauerkraut, lower the heat to low, cover, and simmer for 45 minutes. Bury the slab bacon under the sauerkraut, cover, and simmer for an additional 45 minutes.

4. Cook the potatoes in boiling salted water until soft, about 20 minutes, and then drain.

5. Fill the bottom of a steamer about halfway with water, add the vinegar, and heat to a boil. Season the salmon fillets with salt and pepper, place in the steamer basket, top with the fresh thyme, cover, and steam until just cooked through, 5 to 6 minutes.

6. To serve, spoon a mound of sauerkraut in the center of four plates, top each with a salmon fillet and a slice of slab bacon, surround with potatoes, and serve with coarse sea salt alongside.

PAN-SEARED SEA SCALLOPS *with* CRISP VEGETABLE RISOTTO

° NOIX DE SAINT JACQUES RÔTIES, RISOTTO DE LÉGUMES CROQUANTS °

MAKES 6 SERVINGS

8 tablespoons unsalted butter

1 small zucchini, chopped

1 carrot, chopped

1 turnip, peeled and chopped

1 celery stalk, chopped

1/2 cup chopped celery root

Salt

Freshly ground black pepper

4 cups chicken broth

1 small onion, finely chopped

1 1/2 cups Arborio rice

1/4 cup mascarpone

2 pounds sea scallops

1/2 cup grated Parmigiano-Reggiano

Flat-leaf parsley, for garnish

Extra virgin olive oil

It's the treatment of the vegetables that makes this French take on an Italian dish compelling. Rather than being cooked in a broth and thus sacrificing their taste and texture to it, the vegetables are sautéed just until crisp-tender and added to the risotto once it has absorbed all its broth.

1. Heat 3 tablespoons butter in a saucepan over medium heat, add the zucchini, carrot, turnip, celery, and celery root, season with salt and pepper and cook, stirring frequently, until the vegetables are crisp-tender, 6 to 7 minutes. Transfer the vegetables to a bowl and set aside.

2. Add the broth to the saucepan, heat it to a simmer, and keep warm over very low heat.

3. Heat 2 tablespoons butter in a heavy pot over medium heat. Add the onion and cook, stirring occasionally, until translucent, about 6 minutes. Add the rice and stir until the grains are well coated with butter. Add 1/2 cup of the hot stock and cook, stirring constantly, until all the liquid has been absorbed. Continue to add stock, 1/2 cup at a time, until absorbed, stirring all the time. After 20 minutes, begin to test the rice, which is done when its overall consistency is loose and creamy yet its grains are still firm.

4. Add the cooked vegetables to the risotto and cook, stirring, until heated through, 2 to 3 minutes. Stir in the mascarpone, cover, and turn down the heat to very low.

5. Heat 3 tablespoons butter in a large skillet over high heat. Season the scallops with salt and pepper on both sides and sear just until

golden brown and opaque in the center, 30 seconds to 1 minute per side.

6. To serve, stir the cheese into the risotto, correct the seasoning, and spoon in a mound in the center of six plates. Surround each mound with 4 to 5 scallops, garnish the risotto with parsley, and drizzle the scallops with olive oil.

PAN-SEARED COD *with* POTATO *and* SMOKED SAUSAGE PUREE

◦ DOS DE CABILLAUD POÊLÉ À LA PURÉE DE L'ANDOUILLE DE GUÉMÉMÉ ◦

MAKES 6 SERVINGS

2 pounds Idaho russet
  potatoes

7 tablespoons unsalted
  butter

1 small red onion, finely
  chopped

3 garlic cloves, finely
  chopped

2 tablespoons finely chopped
  shallots

½ cup dry white wine

½ pound smoked sausage,
  thinly sliced

Coarse sea salt

Freshly ground black pepper

3 tablespoons freshly
  squeezed lemon

2 teaspoons grated lemon
  zest

Six 6-ounce cod fillets

3 tablespoons olive oil

2 tablespoons chopped
  chives

When enjoyed hot rather than as a thinly sliced cold cut, andouille de Guémémé *is usually paired with a potato puree that both absorbs and plays off the sausage's pronounced smokiness. The combo is Brittany's version of bangers and mash. Several of the area's chefs have turned the duo into a trio with the addition of a mildly flavored fish such as turbot, bass, or, as in this wine bar recipe from Brittany native Guillaume Dubois, cod. The fish does not have to be cooked with the* andouille *to absorb its intense flavor; it only has to be near it. The fish is essentially smoked by association.* Andouille de Guémémé *is not exported to North America, and its Cajun derivative is too spicy to be a convincing substitute for the original made in the smokehouses of Guémémé-sur-Scorff in northwest France. Count on very satisfying results with your favorite smoked sausage, smoked ham, or chorizo.*

1. Preheat the oven to 300°F. Peel the potatoes, cut them into small cubes, place in a saucepan, cover with cold water, heat to a boil, and cook until tender, about 20 minutes. Drain the potatoes, place in a baking dish or pan, and set in the oven to dry out and stay warm, 10 to 15 minutes.

2. Heat 3 tablespoons butter in a skillet over medium heat. Add the onion, garlic, and shallots and cook, stirring frequently, until the onion is tender and translucent but not brown, 7 to 9 minutes. Raise the heat to moderately high, pour in the wine, and cook, stirring occasionally, just until all the liquid has evaporated, about 5 minutes. Add the smoked sausage and cook, stirring frequently, 5 minutes. Combine this mixture with the potatoes in a large bowl,

season generously with salt and pepper, and mash with a potato masher until reasonably smooth. Cover and keep warm.

3. Combine the lemon juice, lemon zest, and 2 teaspoons water in a saucepan over moderately high heat and heat to a boil. Lower the heat to low and whisk in the remaining butter, 1 tablespoon at a time, until all the butter is incorporated and the sauce coats the back of a spoon. Remove from the heat and cover.

4. Rinse and pat dry the cod fillets and season on both sides with salt and pepper. Heat the olive oil in a skillet over moderately high heat, add the fillets, skin side down, and cook until the skin is crisp and browned, 3 to 4 minutes. Turn the fillets and cook just until cooked through, about 3 minutes.

5. To serve, place a mound of the potatoes and sausage in the center of six plates, flatten each with a spatula, top with a cod fillet, skin side up, sprinkle with chives, and drizzle lemon butter sauce all around.

HOUSE-SALTED COD WRAPPED IN HAM

⊙ MORUE EN JAMBON ⊙

MAKES 4 SERVINGS

4 skinless codfish fillets, 6 to 7 ounces each

2 tablespoons coarse sea salt

¼ to ½ teaspoon piment d'Espelette or ancho powder or other medium-hot chili powder

3 tablespoons olive oil

4 thin slices country ham

Frustrated by the bother and uncertainty of soaking, desalting, and rehydrating dried salt cod in several changes of water over many hours, chefs like Gérard Fouché have taken to salting their own fresh cod. It allows them to have better control over the quality of the fish and the quantity of the salt. Overnight salting gives fresh cod a firmer texture that holds together better when wrapped with ham. Fouché suggests serving the ham-wrapped house-salted cod fillets over eggs pipérade (page 139).

1. The day before you plan to serve: Season the cod fillets on both sides with salt and piment d'Espelette. Place a couple of small plates upside down over a serving plate or tray, lay the fillets over the plates (this will allow the liquid to drain off), cover with plastic wrap, and refrigerate overnight.

2. Preheat the oven to 400°F. Heat the olive oil in a skillet over medium heat. Add the salted cod fillets and cook just until lightly golden, about 1 minute on each side. Drain on paper towels.

3. Working with one slice at a time, spread out the ham, lay a cod fillet over the ham, and roll it, tucking the end of the ham under itself to hold it in place, and transfer to a baking pan. Repeat with the remaining fillets. Place in the oven and bake until just cooked through, 6 to 8 minutes, depending on the thickness of the fillets. Serve atop eggs pipérade, potatoes, or rice.

ROAST WHOLE CHICKEN
with CAULIFLOWER

◦ COUCOU RÔTI DE RENNES, CHOUFLEUR À CRU ◦

MAKES 4 SERVINGS

1 roasting chicken, 5 to 6
 pounds

5 tablespoons unsalted
 butter, softened

Salt

Freshly ground black pepper

1 medium head cauliflower,
 about 1½ pounds

1 small head garlic

5 shallots, quartered

4 carrots, peeled and sliced
 into 1-inch rounds

½ cup coarsely chopped
 hazelnuts

Flat-leaf parsley, for garnish

Behold bistro chef Thierry Breton's tribute to the Coucou de Rennes, *a breed of chicken from his home region of Brittany that is prized for its light hint of hazelnut flavor. He roasts his* coucou *with hazelnuts to accentuate a characteristic you can emulate by basting your chicken of choice with nutty drippings. An additional reward is the pleasing exchange of textures between the chopped hazelnuts and the tender cauliflower. No matter the breed of* coucou *employed, this is one great roast chicken recipe.*

1. Preheat the oven to 425°F. Clean the chicken inside and out with cold water, pat dry with paper towels, and let stand at room temperature for 20 minutes.

2. Smear the butter under the skin and over the outside of the chicken and season thoroughly with salt and pepper. Tie the legs together with kitchen twine, place the chicken, breast side up, in a roasting pan, and cook until the skin begins to crisp, about 20 minutes.

3. Wash the cauliflower and separate it into large florets. Separate the garlic cloves from the head and crush by laying each clove on a flat surface and pressing down on it with the broad side of a large kitchen knife. Distribute the crushed cloves and the shallots around the chicken in the roasting pan, top with the cauliflower and carrots, and drizzle with 1 cup cold water.

4. Lower the oven temperature to 350°F and cook, basting the bird and vegetables with the cooking juices 2 or 3 times, for an additional 20 minutes. Scatter the hazelnuts over the cauliflower and

cook, basting every 10 minutes or so, until the juices run clear when you cut between a leg and a thigh, about 1 hour.

5. Transfer the chicken to a warm serving platter and let stand 10 minutes. Surround the chicken with vegetables, spoon the cooking juices over all, garnish with parsley, and serve immediately, carving the chicken at the table.

POACHED WHOLE CHICKEN *with* CREAM SAUCE

◦ VOLAILLE À LA CRÈME ◦

MAKES 4 SERVINGS

1 pound roasting chicken, 5 to 6 pounds

Salt

Freshly ground black pepper

2 chicken bouillon cubes

2 carrots, peeled and halved

2 onions, peeled and halved

2 turnips, peeled and halved

1 leek, white parts only, washed

2 quarts light cream

Chef David Rathgeber is unapologetic about the quantity of cream that poaches and thoroughly conditions his doubly rich volaille à la crème, *but you can substitute a cup of milk or an additional cup of chicken broth for a cup of the cream and still get a superbly moist and mellow chicken. On the other hand, if this amount of cream concerns you, then this classic probably isn't for you.*

1. Clean the chicken inside and out with cold water, pat dry with paper towels, and let stand at room temperature for 20 minutes. Season liberally with salt and pepper.

2. Dissolve the chicken bouillon cubes in 2 cups boiling water.

3. Preheat the oven to 325°F. Place the chicken in a Dutch oven or ovenproof casserole, add the vegetables, and cover with the bouillon and cream. Heat over moderately high heat just to a boil. Transfer to the oven and cook for about 2 hours.

4. Remove the chicken and vegetables from the casserole, pass 2 to 3 cups of the sauce through a fine sieve into a saucepan, and cook over medium heat, beating with a whisk, until the sauce foams and thickens, about 5 minutes.

5. To serve, cut the chicken in 8 parts. Place the chicken and vegetables on a serving plate and top generously with cream sauce. Serve with Potato "Matafan" (page 135), boiled potatoes, or baked potatoes.

PAN-ROASTED DUCK BREAST
with SPRING VEGETABLES

◦ MAGRET DE CANARD RÔTI, LÉGUMES DE PRINTEMPS AU JUS ◦

MAKES 4 SERVINGS

½ pound baby carrots, trimmed, peeled, and halved if large

½ pound baby turnips, trimmed, peeled, and halved if large

1 cup shelled fresh peas

1 cup shelled fresh fava beans

½ pound pearl onions

4 boneless duck breast halves with skin (about 1½ pounds)

Salt

Freshly ground black pepper

Coarse sea salt

¾ cup chicken stock

7 tablespoons unsalted butter

Flat parsley leaves

Bruno Doucet's systematic recipe for pan-roasted duck breast will have you feeling like an efficient and accomplished bistro cook. The duck breasts render the fat in which they are pan-roasted. The same duck fat subsequently helps prepare and enrich but not overcook the crisp-tender spring vegetables and their silky jus. Even so, the combination of the rendered duck fat and butter, 7 tablespoons of it, is not always sufficiently lush for Doucet's tastes. Before spooning on the buttery jus, he occasionally tops each vertical serving of vegetables and duck breast with a slice of foie gras sautéed in—what else?—its own fat.

1. Cook the vegetables separately in boiling salted water until slightly tender, about 3 minutes for the carrots and turnips, 4 to 5 minutes for the peas and fava beans, and 8 minutes for the pearl onions. Plunge each into ice water to stop the cooking process and set in the color. Drain and set aside.

2. With a sharp knife, carefully trim the skin and fat layer off the duck breast halves, leaving about ¼ inch of fat. Season them on both sides with salt and pepper.

3. Heat a heavy-bottomed saucepan over low heat. Place the duck breast halves in the pan, fat side down, and cook to render off the fat, about 5 minutes. Increase the heat to medium and cook for 7 to 8 minutes. Turn the breasts and cook, spooning juices over them, until the bottoms are lightly browned, about 2 minutes. Transfer the breasts to a plate and tent with aluminum foil.

4. Pour ¼ cup chicken stock into the pan to degrease it and add the butter in small pieces. Once the butter has melted, add the vegetables, raise the heat to moderately high, and cook, stirring, for 3 minutes. Season the vegetables with salt and pepper, add ½ cup chicken stock, let reduce for 1 minute, stir in the parsley, and remove from the heat.

5. To serve, thinly slice the duck breasts at an angle. Using a slotted spoon, transfer the vegetables to four dinner plates, forming a flat mound in the center of each. Top each with duck slices and spoon some of the vegetable *jus* over the meat and vegetables.

PAN-GRILLED RIB STEAK
with BÉARNAISE SAUCE

◦ ENTRECÔTE GRILLÉE, SAUCE BÉARNAISE ◦

MAKES 4 SERVINGS

4 rib steaks (or substitute strip steaks), ¾ inch thick, 8 to 10 ounces each

4 tablespoons soybean or grapeseed oil

2 tablespoons unsalted butter

Salt

Freshly ground black pepper

Béarnaise Sauce (recipe follows)

When it comes to steaks, Parisian bistro chefs invariably prefer the sizzling sear of a frypan to a charcoal or wood-fired grill. The superiority of Thierry Laurent's steaks is immediately apparent in their color and luster: The blackened steaks have a reddish sheen you can reproduce, by first warming the steaks to room temperature, using a nonstick skillet so that not much oil and butter are required, using an oil such as grapeseed or soybean with a high smoking point, and adding the butter just before the steaks so it does not brown. It does not hurt any to serve them with Laurent's incomparable béarnaise sauce and frites *(page 138). The béarnaise, in addition to being the definitive accompaniment for steak frites, may also be served with fried, broiled, or grilled fish, especially salmon; Cold Bœuf à la Ficelle with Spring Vegetables and Horseradish (page 102), roast beef; broiled chicken; egg dishes; and vegetables (asparagus, artichoke hearts).*

1. Remove the steaks from the refrigerator 30 to 60 minutes before cooking them.

2. Heat 2 tablespoons soybean oil in 2 large nonstick skillets over high heat until very hot. Drop 1 tablespoon butter in each pan, immediately add the steaks, and sear for 3 minutes (for medium rare). Turn the steaks, season the cooked sides with salt and pepper, and sear the uncooked sides for 3 minutes.

3. Turn the steaks onto plates, season with salt and pepper, and serve immediately with béarnaise sauce (served at room temperature in four small cups or ramekins) and, ideally, *frites.*

BÉARNAISE SAUCE
(sauce béarnaise)

....

1/4 cup red wine vinegar

1/4 cup dry white wine

1 tablespoon finely chopped
   shallots

3 tablespoons finely chopped
   fresh tarragon

Pinch of salt

1/4 teaspoon crushed black
   pepper

1/2 cup (1 stick) butter

3 egg yolks

Freshly ground black pepper

1. Combine the vinegar, white wine, shallots, 2 tablespoons tarragon, the salt, crushed black pepper, and 1/4 cup water in a saucepan over medium heat and heat until the liquid is reduced to 3 tablespoons, 10 to 12 minutes. Remove from the heat and let cool.

2. Meanwhile, clarify the butter by placing it in a saucepan over low heat until melted. Skim off and discard the foamy white milk solids that form on the surface and set the clear liquid aside.

3. Set the saucepan with the vinegar-and-wine reduction over very low heat and add the egg yolks, one at a time, beating vigorously with a whisk in a figure 8 pattern until the foamy mixture thickens and you can see the bottom of the pan between strokes, 4 to 5 minutes. Remove from the heat and very slowly whisk in the melted butter (leaving the white solids in the pan), drop by drop, beating constantly until fully incorporated. If the finished sauce breaks apart or separates, whisk in 1 tablespoon cold water to smooth it. Strain the sauce through a fine sieve, add the remaining 1 tablespoon tarragon, and season to taste with salt and freshly ground black pepper. Once cool, transfer to a lidded jar or container, and store in the refrigerator for at least 3 hours and up to 2 days. Remove from the refrigerator about 30 minutes before serving.

COLD BŒUF À LA FICELLE *with* SPRING VEGETABLES *and* HORSERADISH

◦ BŒUF À LA FICELLE GLACÉ, LÉGUMES NOUVEAUX AU RAIFORT ◦

MAKES 6 SERVINGS

3 onions, halved

1 clove

2 tablespoons olive oil

¾ pound boneless beef (chuck, shank, or short ribs), cut into 2-inch cubes

2 pounds veal bones or chicken parts

5 carrots, peeled

2 celery stalks

1 leek, white parts only

4 garlic cloves

10 to 12 black peppercorns

Salt

½ pound haricots verts, ends clipped

2 cups shelled fresh peas or frozen peas

½ pound turnips, peeled and cut into 1-inch cubes

2 pounds boneless rib-eye roast, rib roast, or rump roast

Coarse sea salt

Rodolphe Paquin reinterprets the boiled beef classic bœuf à la ficelle *("beef on a string") as a summer bistro dish by cooking the beef a day in advance and chilling it overnight in its gelatinous broth. Whatever the month and climate, try both the first-day and second-day versions. Served warm, the pristine slices of deep pink beef possess the purity of a carpaccio or a Vietnamese boiled beef. No pot au feu or roast beef ever tasted like this. When chilled, it slices beautifully into a cold beef dish of unparalleled elegance. Though the* bœuf à la ficelle, *as its name implies, is customarily prepared by tying the beef with string, wrapping the ends of that string around the handles of a stockpot, and suspending the meat in its poaching broth, it's perfectly okay if you forgo the suspending part and let the beef sit in the broth, providing you turn it once while it cooks.*

1. Place the onion halves, cut side down, in a nonstick skillet and cook over low heat until the bottoms are golden brown, about 5 minutes. Remove from the heat and stick the clove into one of them.

2. Heat the olive oil in a large stockpot over medium heat, add the boneless chuck, shank, or short ribs, and brown on all sides, 3 to 4 minutes. Add the veal bones or chicken parts, 2 carrots, celery, leek, garlic, and black peppercorns, cover with 2½ quarts cold water, season with salt, and bring to a boil over medium-high heat. Cover the pot, lower the heat to very low, and cook at a gentle simmer for 2 hours. Strain the solids (reserve the beef and vegetables to prepare as a separate leftover stew, reheated in the beef stock left over from this recipe), return the stock to the pot, raise the heat to medium-high and heat to a boil.

Horseradish sauce, Dijon mustard, or Béarnaise Sauce (page 101)

Cornichons, optional

3. Cut the remaining carrots into 1-inch slices. Add to the stock along with the haricots verts, peas, and turnips and cook for 15 minutes. Securely tie the beef both lengthwise and crosswise with string. Submerge the beef in the stock, reduce the heat to low, cover, and simmer, turning once, 18 to 20 minutes for rare, 22 to 24 minutes for medium rare. Lift the meat from the stock and remove the stock and vegetables from the heat.

4. If serving hot, untie the beef and carve it into thin slices as you would a roast beef, arranging them along with the drained vegetables on a large serving platter. Serve with coarse sea salt, horseradish sauce, Dijon mustard, or béarnaise sauce, and cornichons, if desired.

5. If serving cold, remove the beef from the stock to a large platter and let it cool. Then combine it with the stock and the vegetables in a large bowl or container, cover with plastic wrap, and refrigerate for up to 3 days. To serve, remove the beef and vegetables from the gelatinous stock (reserving the stock for future use), carve the beef into thin slices, and serve with the same accompaniments.

Rodolphe Paquin unwinds with some habitués at Le Repaire de Cartouche.

PAN-FRIED STEAKS *with* MUSTARD CREAM SAUCE

◦ PAVÉS DU MAIL ◦

MAKES 4 SERVINGS

4 sirloin or rib-eye steaks, ¾ inch thick, 8 to 10 ounces each

2 tablespoons unsalted butter

2 tablespoons vegetable oil

¼ cup Cognac or fine brandy

¼ cup light whipping cream

4 teaspoons Dijon mustard

Salt

Freshly ground black pepper

These classic bistro-style steaks take their name from the rue du Mail. You may flambé the Cognac for purposes of showmanship, but this is hardly required. The steak au poivre variation, though not exactly the same as the Chez Georges rendition, will not yield a single regret.

1. Remove the steaks from the refrigerator 30 to 45 minutes before cooking them. Pat them dry with paper towels.

2. Heat the butter and oil in a large skillet over moderately high heat until hot but not smoking and cook the steaks to desired doneness, about 4 minutes on each side for medium rare. Transfer the steaks to a warm platter and cover to keep warm.

3. Pull the skillet away from the heat and pour in the Cognac to deglaze it. Stir with a wooden spatula or spoon, scraping up burnt bits from the bottom with a wooden spoon, until the liquid is reduced by half, 20 to 30 seconds. Return the skillet to the heat, add the cream and mustard, season with salt and pepper, and simmer, stirring the sauce with a whisk until it thickens, about 1 minute. Stir in any meat juices that have drained from the steaks onto the warm platter.

4. To serve, spoon the sauce liberally over the steaks.

Steak au poivre: Before cooking the steaks, increase the quantity of Cognac to ½ cup, pour it in a large plate or shallow bowl, and let each steak soak in it for 1 minute on each side. Spread ¼ cup crushed black pepper in another plate, roll each steak in the pepper to fully coat on both sides, and set aside for 10 minutes. Then follow the recipe above, halving the quantity of Dijon mustard.

SHEPHERD'S PIE

⊙ HACHIS PARMENTIER ⊙

MAKES 6 SERVINGS

2 pounds boneless beef, preferably a mixture of bottom round, pot roast, or rump roast

4 onions

1 clove

Bouquet garni (1 bay leaf, 1 sprig fresh thyme, 3 sprigs fresh parsley)

2 carrots, peeled

2 shallots, sliced

4 garlic cloves, crushed

½ teaspoon black peppercorns

1 teaspoon sea salt

2 pounds Idaho russet potatoes

2 tablespoons butter, plus butter for the pan

1 cup milk

1 tablespoon light whipping cream

2 tablespoons olive oil

½ pound coarse pork sausage, removed from casings

This bistro's acclaimed hachis parmentier *is almost too good to prepare with meat from a leftover* pot au feu, *as is customary. Not that there's anything wrong with doing so: A hachis made with leftover stew makes mincemeat out of versions made with prepackaged ground beef, but it would be nice to elevate this classic to first-night status.*

1. Place the beef in a stockpot, cover with 2½ quarts cold water, and heat over high heat to a boil. Skim off any foam that rises to the surface.

2. Spear 1 onion with the clove and add it to the stockpot, along with the bouquet garni, carrots, shallots, garlic, peppercorns, and sea salt. Lower the heat to low and cook at a simmer, skimming occasionally and adding a little water as necessary, for 4 hours.

3. An hour or so before the beef is done, peel the potatoes, cut them into small cubes, place in a saucepan, cover with cold salted water, heat to a boil, and cook until tender, about 20 minutes. Drain the potatoes, pass through a food mill or mash them with a potato masher, and return to the saucepan over low heat. Add the butter, little by little, stirring constantly with a wooden spoon. Meanwhile, heat the milk and cream together in a separate pan and slowly stir into the potatoes. Remove from the heat and cover to keep warm.

4. Turn off the heat under the stockpot, remove the meat (reserving the bouillon), cut it into small pieces, and let cool. Grind the meat in a food processor.

5. Preheat the oven to 375°F. Butter a 1½-quart baking dish or gratin dish. Chop the remaining onions. Heat the olive oil in a saucepan over low heat, add the onions and sweat them, stirring fre-

Salt

Freshly ground black pepper

½ cup grated Parmigiano-Reggiano

quently, until very soft, about 15 minutes. Add the sausage and cook, stirring frequently, for 10 minutes. Stir in the ground beef and 1½ cups bouillon from the stockpot and season with salt and pepper.

6. Spread the meat mixture in an even layer on the bottom of the prepared dish. Top with an even layer of mashed potatoes, cover with an even layer of grated cheese, and bake just until the top turns golden brown, 20 to 25 minutes. Serve immediately with a salad of mixed greens.

SAUERKRAUT *with* PORK *and* SAUSAGES

° CHOUCROUTE GARNIE °

MAKES 8 SERVINGS

2 pounds smoked ham hocks

Salt

3 tablespoons lard or
    vegetable oil

3 onions, thinly sliced

1 tart apple (Granny
    Smith), peeled, cored, and
    thinly sliced

3 pounds unsweetened
    sauerkraut (see page 88)

2 cups dry white wine

1 tablespoon juniper berries

1½ teaspoons black
    peppercorns

2 bay leaves

3 sprigs fresh thyme

½ pound piece slab bacon

2 tablespoons vegetable oil

1 pound smoked boneless
    pork loin (Canadian
    bacon), thickly sliced

4 precooked bratwurst or
    kielbasa

4 frankfurters

16 small to medium red
    bliss potatoes

Freshly ground black pepper

Dijon mustard

My recipe for the definitive brasserie dish, though inspired by Bofinger, does not come from one single kitchen or chef. It is a composite and somewhat simplified adaptation calling for store-bought sauerkraut as well as pork and sausages readily available in North American markets. Ideally, choucroute should be served with an Alsatian white wine or cold beer.

1. Place the ham hocks in a large pot, cover with water, season with a little salt, and bring to a boil. Lower the heat to low, cover, and simmer for 2 hours. Drain the ham hocks, reserving 1 cup of the broth.

2. Heat the lard in a 5-quart casserole over medium heat, add the onions and apple and cook, stirring occasionally, until the onions are translucent but not colored, 7 to 9 minutes. Add the sauerkraut and ham hocks, cover with the wine and ham hock broth, and season with a pinch of salt.

3. Wrap the juniper berries, peppercorns, bay leaves, and fresh thyme in a cheesecloth, add this sack to the sauerkraut, lower the heat to low, cover, and cook for 30 minutes. Bury the slab bacon under the sauerkraut and cook for another 30 minutes.

4. Heat the vegetable oil in a skillet over medium heat. Add the pork loin and cook until lightly browned on all sides, about 2 minutes per side. Remove the pork loin and brown the bratwurst and the frankfurters in the same skillet. Bury the pork loin, bratwurst, and frankfurters under the sauerkraut and braise the pork for another 30 to 45 minutes.

5. Meanwhile, cook the potatoes in boiling salted water until soft, about 20 minutes, and drain and slice them in two.

THE BISTROS, BRASSERIES, AND WINE BARS OF PARIS ° *107*

6. Remove the cheesecloth sack from the sauerkraut and season to taste with salt and pepper.

7. To serve, slice the bacon and sausage. Transfer the sauerkraut to a large serving platter, arrange all the meats on top, surround with the halved potatoes, and serve with mustard.

BOILED PICNIC HAM
with GREEN LENTILS

◦ PALETTE DE PORC DEMI-SEL AUX LENTILLES VERTES DE PUY ◦

MAKES 6 SERVINGS

One 5 to 6-pound picnic
  ham

2 onions

4 whole cloves

1 carrot, peeled

1 leek, white parts only

2 teaspoons black
  peppercorns

1 celery stalk

5 to 6 cups chicken stock

3 tablespoons lard or
  unsalted butter

1 cup chopped shallots

6 ounces slab bacon, diced

2 cups French green lentils,
  washed and drained

1 hard-boiled egg, chopped

3 tablespoons chopped flat-
  leaf parsley

1 teaspoon minced
  (drained) capers

1 cornichon or baby gherkin,
  minced

1 tablespoon Dijon mustard

At Le Beurre Noisette and other bistros, the partiality toward the palette de porc demi-sel *(salt-cured upper shoulder of pork) is the same as that which makes the portion American butchers know as Boston butt ideal for pulled pork barbecue: ample fat.* Palette de porc demi-sel, *a key component of* choucroute garnie *and traditional meat soups known as* potées, *is widely available in French markets. The best American stand-in for it, short of salt-curing your own* palette, *is picnic ham. If substituting a leaner boneless country ham, you'll only need about half the weight to serve six people.*

Thierry Blanqui applies the risotto cooking technique to the French green lentils of Puy, first toasting them lightly in a little lard to preserve their round shape and fine skin and then simmering them in broth added in small quantities until tender but still a little al dente or croquant *(crunchy).*

The dip for the meat is a ravigote, *a vinaigrette thickened and seasoned with minced capers, a gherkin, and shallots and traditionally served at room temperature with boiled meats or fish.*

1. The day before: Soak the picnic ham overnight in cold water to reduce its saltiness and smokiness.

2. Drain the ham, scrub it with a stiff brush, place it in a large pot or Dutch oven in which the meat fits fairly snugly, cover with cold water, and heat over high heat to a rapid boil. Skim off the foam that has risen to the surface.

3. Pierce 1 onion with 3 whole cloves and add it to the pot, along with the carrot, leek, peppercorns, and celery. Lower the heat to low and simmer, partly covered, adding water as needed, until a meat thermometer shows an internal temperature of 150 to 155°F, 2½ to

½ cup vegetable oil

1 tablespoon red wine
vinegar

Salt

Freshly ground black pepper

3 hours (25 minutes per pound of ham). When done, the meat will start to separate from the bone and show little resistance when stuck with a knife. Turn off the heat and let cool in the liquid for 1 hour. Remove from the pot about 20 minutes before carving.

4. To prepare the lentils: Heat the chicken stock in a saucepan just to a boil, lower the heat to very low, and keep at a gentle simmer.

5. Melt the lard in a large saucepan over medium heat. Add ¾ cup of the chopped shallots and sweat, stirring occasionally with a wooden spoon and not letting them color, for 3 minutes. Add the bacon and cook, stirring occasionally, for 2 minutes. Add the lentils and cook, stirring constantly, for 3 minutes. Cover the lentils with 2 cups chicken stock and simmer, stirring constantly and adjusting the heat as necessary, until the liquid has been absorbed. Continue to add hot stock, 1 cup at a time, and cook, stirring constantly, until each successive batch has been absorbed. Begin to taste the lentils after 30 minutes of simmering. Once the lentils are tender yet still firm, boil off whatever liquid remains, cover the saucepan, and remove from the heat.

6. To prepare the *ravigote* sauce: Mince the remaining ¼ cup chopped shallots. Combine them with the hard-boiled egg, 1 tablespoon parsley, capers, and gherkin in a small bowl and mix well. In a separate bowl, prepare a vinaigrette: Combine the mustard, vegetable oil, and vinegar and beat with a whisk. Add the egg mixture to the vinaigrette and mix well.

7. To serve, carve the ham into thin slices. Season the lentils to taste with salt and pepper, spoon a mound of lentils in the center of six plates, sprinkle each with the remaining chopped parsley, lay the ham slices over the lentils, and serve with the *ravigote* sauce spooned into six small ramekins or dipping cups.

ROAST LOIN OF VEAL
with FRESH ROSEMARY

❀ QUASI DE VEAU AU ROMARIN ❀

MAKES 4 SERVINGS

1 boneless loin of veal roast,
  about 2½ pounds, tied
  into a compact cylinder

Salt

Freshly ground black pepper

2 tablespoons olive oil

2 tablespoons unsalted
  butter

1 tablespoon chopped fresh
  rosemary

2 garlic cloves, chopped

It's not required that you serve Thierry Blanqui's exquisitely unfussy veal roast and its sublime rosemary garlic jus *alongside his Celery Root Puree (page 131), but once you try them together, you won't tolerate them apart.*

1. Preheat the oven to 325°F. Season the veal with salt and pepper. Heat the olive oil in a Dutch oven or ovenproof casserole over medium heat. Add the veal and cook, turning it with tongs, until brown on all sides, 8 to 10 minutes. Remove from the heat.

2. Spread the butter over the top of the veal roast, sprinkle the meat with the rosemary, and insert an ovenproof meat thermometer so its tip is centered in the thickest part. Roast in the oven, basting 2 or 3 times with the juices in the casserole, until the thermometer registers 155°F (the meat will continue to cook while standing to about 160°F, its ideal temperature), about 1½ hours. Remove the meat from the casserole and transfer to a warm platter.

3. Pour or spoon off most of the greasy meat juices from the casserole and then place the casserole with the remaining juices over medium heat. Add the garlic and enough cold water to fill about ½ inch of the pan and heat to a boil. Cook until the liquid has thickened slightly and reduced by half, 2 to 3 minutes, being careful that the quickly evaporating liquid does not boil away. If it does, just add more water and reduce again. Remove from the heat and season, if necessary, with additional salt and pepper.

4. To serve, remove the string from the veal roast, carve it into thick slices, and spoon cooking juices over them.

VEAL BLANQUETTE *with* GINGER *and* LEMONGRASS

◦ BLANQUETTE DE VEAU AUX ÉPICES ◦

3 pounds breast of veal or
  other stew meat, cut into
  2-inch pieces

Salt

Freshly ground black pepper

2 tablespoons butter

2 tablespoons vegetable oil

4 carrots, peeled and cut
  into ½-inch slices

1 pound mushrooms, sliced

2 onions, sliced

2 tablespoons chopped
  lemongrass

2 tablespoons lemon zest

1 tablespoon curry powder

One 2-inch piece fresh
  ginger, peeled and thinly
  sliced

½ cinnamon stick

1½ to 2 quarts chicken
  stock

2 egg yolks

2 tablespoons heavy cream

3 tablespoons lemon juice

*Raquel Carena invigorates this classic white-sauced stew by
disposing of its flour, reducing its cream content, and adding
lemongrass, lemon zest, and ginger. The Asian accent may upset some
French purists, but not likely those who have sampled this aromatic
version at Carena's wine bar. The blanquette keeps its rustic
identity—it's hearty bistro cooking, there's no question about that—
and yet its flavors are crisp, lively, and sophisticated.*

1. Preheat the oven to 300°F. Season the veal pieces with salt and
pepper. Heat the butter and oil in a Dutch oven or ovenproof casserole over medium-high heat. Cook the veal in batches, turning occasionally and adding a little oil between batches if the casserole gets
dry, until the meat is browned on all sides, about 5 minutes per
batch. Transfer the veal to a plate.

2. Place the carrots, mushrooms, onions, lemongrass, lemon zest,
curry, ginger, and cinnamon stick in the casserole, lower the heat to
medium, and cook, stirring frequently, until the vegetables begin to
soften but do not brown, 6 to 8 minutes. Remove from the heat.

3. Add the meat, pour in just enough chicken stock to cover the
meat, season with salt and pepper, and cook in the oven, covered,
for 2 hours. Raise the heat to 400°F, uncover the casserole, and
cook for an additional 30 minutes. Remove from the oven, let cool,
and refrigerate for up to 24 hours.

4. About 30 minutes before serving, lift and discard the fat from the
stew and reheat it slowly over medium heat to a simmer. Cover, simmer for an additional 5 minutes, and then remove from the heat.

5. Combine the egg yolks and cream and beat with a whisk. Gradually beat in the lemon juice, pour the mixture into the casserole, and combine with the rest of the stew. Set over medium heat, gently shaking the casserole, and making sure it does not come to a simmer until the sauce has thickened slightly. Serve with rice.

Philippe Pinoteau serves up bon vins *and* bon mots *at Le Baratin.*

CURRIED LAMB STEW

◦ CURRY D'AGNEAU ◦

MAKES 6 SERVINGS

3 pounds boneless lamb
stew meat, preferably
shoulder

3 tablespoons vegetable oil

1 banana, sliced

2 apples, preferably Golden
Delicious, peeled, cored,
and cut into chunks

1 onion, chopped

2 garlic cloves, chopped

2 tablespoons curry powder

1/2 to 1 teaspoon cayenne
pepper

2 tablespoons dried coconut

3/4 cup flour

2 cups crushed tomatoes

3 tablespoons chopped
curly-leaf parsley

1 bouquet garni (1 bay leaf,
1 sprig fresh thyme,
3 sprigs fresh parsley)

Salt

Freshly ground black pepper

2 tablespoons unsalted
butter

Achards aux légumes,
optional (page 141)

The origins of brasserie classics described as "Eastern" are generally no farther afield than the French border region of Alsace. Such Alsatian specialties as choucroute and kouglof are, in fact, about as foreign as nineteenth- and twentieth-century French brasserie cooking got. La Coupole's introduction of curry d'agneau *soon after its 1927 opening thus constituted a jolt comparable to the most radical works produced by artists then colonizing Montparnasse and its famous cafés. The curry, with its strange spices, chutneys, and accompaniments, was served from a cart wheeled around the dining room by a dashing Madras in his native costume. The theatrical presentation disappeared many years ago, perhaps because the dish had already lost much of its exoticism. It is now a familiar and integral part not only of brasserie tradition but also of French cookery.*

1. Cut the lamb into 2-inch cubes and pat dry with paper towels.

2. Heat the oil in a large casserole over moderately high heat. Add the lamb, banana, and half the apple chunks and cook, turning, until the meat is browned on all sides, about 5 minutes. Remove the lamb and fruit with a slotted spoon onto a paper towel–lined plate.

3. Add the onion and garlic to the casserole, lower the heat to medium, and cook, stirring occasionally, until the onion is translucent, about 5 minutes.

4. Return the lamb and fruit to the casserole. Mix in the curry powder, cayenne, and coconut and cook, stirring continuously, for 2 minutes. Mix in the flour and cook, stirring continuously so the flour does not stick to the pan, for an additional 2 minutes.

5. Add the tomatoes, parsley, and bouquet garni, season with salt and pepper, and pour in just enough cold water to cover the lamb cubes. Cover, lower the heat to low, and simmer for 90 minutes.

6. Just before you're ready to serve, melt the butter in a saucepan over medium heat, add the remaining apple chunks, and cook, tossing occasionally, until they're softened but not mushy, 4 to 5 minutes. Add to the lamb curry, adjust the seasoning, and serve with rice and, if desired, achards, Indian-style vegetable pickles.

Chef d'Orchestre: *Paul Delbard calls out cues in the kitchen of La Coupole.*

GRILLED LAMB STEAKS *with* GARLIC BUTTER *and* POTATO GRATIN

◦ TRANCHE DE GIGOT GRILLÉE, BEURRE À L'AIL, GRATIN DAUPHINOIS ◦

MAKES 4 SERVINGS

2 tablespoons chopped fresh parsley

4 garlic cloves, chopped

4 tablespoons unsalted butter

4 lamb leg steaks or lamb chops, each about ½ pound and ¾ to 1 inch thick

2 tablespoons olive oil

Salt

Freshly ground black pepper

How do you improve upon the basic yet unbeatable idea of grilled lamb topped with garlic butter? By serving it, as this brasserie does, alongside the creamiest potato gratin (recipe follows) and most fragrant Provençal Tomatoes with Thyme (page 128).

1. Combine the parsley and garlic in a small bowl, cover, and refrigerate until ready to prepare the butter sauce.

2. Melt the butter in a small saucepan over low heat, add the parsley-garlic mixture, and cook for 3 minutes. Reduce the heat to very low and cover to keep warm.

3. Prepare a medium-hot charcoal fire in a grill, preheat a gas grill, or heat a lightly oiled grill pan over moderately high heat until hot but not smoking. Brush the lamb steaks on both sides with the olive oil, season with salt and the pepper, and grill them, turning once, 3 to 4 minutes on each side for medium-rare. Transfer to a warm serving platter and let rest a couple of minutes before serving.

4. To serve, spoon the parsley-garlic butter sauce over each lamb steak.

POTATO GRATIN
(gratin dauphinois)

....

2 pounds Idaho russet
  potatoes, peeled and cut
  into ⅛-inch-thick rounds

Butter, for the baking dish

1 to 2 garlic cloves, chopped

Small pinch of nutmeg

Salt

Freshly ground black pepper

2 cups heavy cream

1 cup (4 ounces) grated
  Gruyère

Preheat the oven to 400°F and generously butter a 2-quart baking or gratin dish. Arrange the potato rounds in flat, even layers in the prepared dish, top with the garlic, sprinkle with nutmeg, season with salt and pepper, cover with the cream, and bake in the oven until the potatoes are tender, 45 to 50 minutes. Sprinkle the grated cheese evenly over the top of the gratin and continue to bake until the top is golden, 10 to 15 minutes. Remove from the oven and let cool for 5 to 10 minutes before serving.

LAMB-STUFFED EGGPLANT PARMESAN

◦ CAPILOTADE D'AGNEAU EN PEAU D'AUBERGINE GRATINÉE AU PARMESAN ◦

MAKES 4 SERVINGS

2 tablespoons vegetable oil

1 pound lamb bones

1 small onion, chopped

1 small carrot, peeled and chopped

1 celery stalk, chopped

½ cup dry white wine

2 tablespoons chopped fresh rosemary

2 tablespoons chopped fresh thyme

1 bay leaf

8 to 10 garlic cloves, chopped

Salt

Freshly ground black pepper

¾ cup olive oil

Pinch of coarse sea salt

4 eggplant (8 to 10 ounces each), halved lengthwise

1 pound Yukon gold or Idaho russet potatoes, peeled and cut into ½-inch cubes

2 pounds lamb shoulder, cut into ½-inch cubes

A capilotade is usually a hash or, since it's typically made with leftover meats, a rehash cooked nearly to the point of disintegration. The wonder of the example François Pasteau prepares at his bistro is that the potatoes within the lamb and eggplant ragout maintain some of their firmness. A crisp salad topped with a simple vinaigrette makes a nice accompaniment for these velvety stuffed eggplant. The lamb may be prepared in advance.

1. To prepare the lamb stock: Heat the vegetable oil in a stockpot over medium-high heat, add the lamb bones, and cook, tossing occasionally, until browned, about 5 minutes. Add the onion, carrot, and celery and cook, stirring often, just until the onions turn golden, 4 to 5 minutes. Pour the wine into the pot to degrease it, cover with 2 quarts water, add 1 tablespoon chopped rosemary, 1 tablespoon chopped thyme, the bay leaf, and half the chopped garlic, season with salt and pepper, and heat to a boil. Lower the heat to very low, cover partially, and gently simmer, skimming frequently, for 2 hours. Strain the stock through a fine strainer, pressing on the bones and vegetables to squeeze out all their flavor. Heat the strained stock over medium-high heat until reduced by one-third, 20 to 25 minutes.

2. Preheat the oven to 400°F. Cover the bottom of a large roasting pan with ¼ to ⅓ cup olive oil and sprinkle with coarse sea salt and the remaining rosemary and thyme. Place the eggplant halves in the pan, cut side down, and roast until tender, 45 minutes. Remove from the oven and set aside just until cool enough to handle. Scoop out the pulp from the eggplant halves with a spoon, being careful not to pierce or tear the skins (save the roasting pan for later).

2 tablespoons chopped tarragon

¼ pound shaved Parmigiano-Reggiano

3. Cook the potatoes in boiling salted water just until the cubes begin to soften, 12 to 15 minutes (they will finish cooking with the lamb).

4. Raise the oven temperature to 425°F. Heat 3 tablespoons olive oil in a saucepan over high heat, add the lamb cubes, and cook, tossing frequently, until browned on all sides, 3 to 5 minutes. Discard the fat from the pan. Pour in enough lamb stock to rise about ½ inch over the level of the meat and cook until the stock is reduced to the level of the meat, 10 to 15 minutes. Add the remaining chopped garlic, the tarragon, and eggplant pulp and quickly heat to a boil. Add the potato cubes, lower the heat, and simmer for 15 minutes. Remove from the heat and let cool.

5. Carefully spoon the lamb mixture into the eggplant skins, smoothing the tops. Place them side by side in the roasting pan, top with the Parmesan shavings, drizzle with olive oil, and bake until the stuffing is puffed and the cheese is melted, about 20 minutes. Divide the 8 stuffed halves among four plates and serve.

POTATO GNOCCHI *with* CHESTNUTS, BACON, *and* FRESH HERBS

◦ GNOCCHI DE POMME DE TERRE, CHÂTAIGNE, LARD, ET HERBES FINES ◦

MAKES 6 APPETIZER
SERVINGS OR 4 MAIN-
COURSE SERVINGS
(18 TO 20 GNOCCHI)

1 pound Idaho russet
   potatoes

1⅓ cups flour

1 egg yolk

Salt

Freshly ground black pepper

6 chestnuts

4 strips bacon, chopped

2 tablespoons chopped
   thyme

2 tablespoons chopped
   rosemary

2 tablespoons chopped
   chives

1 teaspoon olive oil

4 tablespoons butter

1½ cups chicken stock

3 to 4 shallots, thinly sliced

Stéphane Jégo ordinarily prepares his bistro's gnocchi with foie gras and was not initially thrilled by my suggestion to substitute bacon for it in this home version (raw foie gras is not readily available in Parisian supermarkets, much less North American ones). This variation does, however, preserve two crucial characteristics reflecting his rustic but original approach to bistro cooking: First, the ingredients—chestnut, bacon, herbs—hidden within the gnocchi reappear in the sauce. You see what they're made of. Jégo and other chefs deconstruct their soups in a similar manner, serving the solids on the bottom of a bowl before a pureed soup made with some of those solids is ladled atop them. Second, the very late addition and minimal cooking of the shallots preserves their mild pungency and invigorates the dish.

1. Put the unpeeled potatoes in a pot, cover with cold salted water, and bring to a boil. Simmer until tender, 35 to 40 minutes. Drain, let stand until just cool enough to handle, peel, and puree with a ricer or food mill into a large mixing bowl. (You may also use a potato masher, being careful not to leave any lumps.) Add the flour and egg yolk, season with salt and pepper, and mix well.

2. Using a sharp pointed knife, slash a large X along the flat sides of the chestnuts. Place them in a saucepan, cover with cold water, heat to a boil, and simmer for 3 minutes. Remove from the heat and peel off the shells and skins of the chestnuts with a sharp knife. Once all the chestnuts have been peeled, chop them.

3. Combine the chestnuts, bacon, thyme, and rosemary in a bowl and mix well so that the ingredients are evenly distributed. Add half this mixture to the potato-flour mixture, reserving the remainder for the sauce. Add 1 tablespoon chopped chives to the potato mixture

and mix well. Shape and roll with your hands into smooth, tightly packed balls 1 ½ to 2 inches in diameter and flatten each a little with the back of a spatula to form the gnocchi.

4. Bring a large pot of salted water to a rapid boil, add the olive oil and then the gnocchi, and cook until they all rise to the surface, about 3 minutes. Plunge into cold water to stop the cooking, drain, and pat dry.

5. Heat the butter in a large skillet over medium heat until it foams but does not brown. Add the gnocchi and cook, turning once, until they're lightly browned, 2 to 3 minutes on each side. Add the chicken stock and the remainder of the chestnut-bacon-herb mixture and cook until the liquid is reduced by half, 4 to 5 minutes. In the last 30 seconds, add the shallots and the remaining chives. Serve immediately, dividing the gnocchi among four plates and spooning the sauce over them.

PROVENÇAL-STYLE STUFFED VEGETABLES

◦ PETITS FARÇIS DE PROVENCE ◦

MAKES 4 SERVINGS

2 small eggplant

Salt

4 small onions

2 zucchini

4 small to medium tomatoes

4 small red or green bell
   peppers

6 to 8 tablespoons olive oil

3 garlic cloves, crushed

¼ pound coarse pork
   sausage, casings removed

¼ pound ground beef

Freshly ground black pepper

1 cup dry red wine

¼ cup grated Parmigiano-
   Reggiano

3 slices white bread, cut or
   torn into tiny pieces

2 eggs, beaten

3 tablespoons chopped fresh
   flat-leaf parsley

½ cup bread crumbs

Lipp serves its commendably simple version of this Provençal classic as a plat du jour. Petits farçis *means "small stuffed," the vegetables being understood.*

1. Halve the eggplant lengthwise and scoop out the pulp with a teaspoon, leaving shells at least ¼ inch thick. Chop the pulp and set aside. Sprinkle the shells with salt and turn them, cut side down, over paper towels to drain.

2. Cut the tops off the onions and a very thin slice off their bottoms. Peel the onions and, using the point of a knife and a teaspoon, remove the center of the onions, leaving a shell at least ⅓ inch thick. Chop the onions removed from the middle and set aside. Cook the outer shells in boiling salted water until slightly softened, about 5 minutes. Drain and set aside.

3. Cut off the ends of the zucchini and cook the zucchini in boiling salted water until just tender, about 6 minutes. Drain, cut the zucchini in half lengthwise, and scoop out the pulp with a melon baller or apple corer, leaving a shell about ¼ inch thick. Chop the pulp and set aside.

4. Cut a ¼ inch slice from the top of each tomato. Discard the tops. Gently scoop out the pulp with a teaspoon, being careful not to pierce the skin. Chop the pulp and set aside.

5. Make a circular incision around the stems of the bell peppers and remove the stems and the seeds and white membranes inside.

6. Preheat the oven to 375°F. Heat 3 tablespoons olive oil in a saucepan over medium heat. Add the chopped onions and garlic

and cook until the onions are softened, 5 minutes. Add the pulp of the remaining vegetables and then the sausage and ground beef, season with salt and pepper, and cook, stirring occasionally, until the meat is browned, 3 to 5 minutes. Add the red wine, lower the heat, and simmer, stirring occasionally, until the liquid has evaporated. Remove from the heat, add the cheese, bread pieces, eggs, and parsley and mix well.

7. Fill the vegetables with this stuffing, mounding it slightly, sprinkle with bread crumbs, place in a greased baking dish, drizzle all with olive oil, and bake until the tops of the stuffed vegetables are golden, 40 to 45 minutes. Serve immediately.

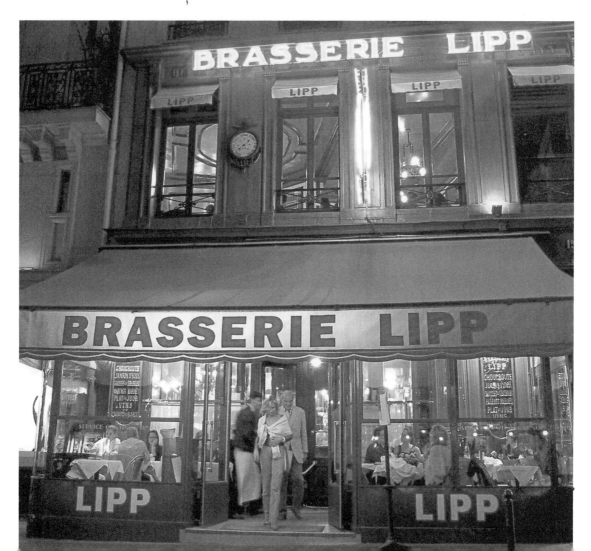

MIXED GRILL OF MARKET VEGETABLES

◦ PARRILLADA DE TOUS LES LÉGUMES DU MARCHÉ ◦

MAKES 4 MAIN-COURSE
SERVINGS

1 pound Idaho russet or
Yukon gold potatoes,
peeled and cut into ½-inch
slices

4 carrots, peeled and cut
into ½-inch slices

1 pound asparagus,
trimmed

1 garlic clove, halved

¼ cup chopped fresh thyme

Salt

Freshly ground black pepper

2 small eggplant, cut into
½-inch slices

2 zucchini, cut into ½-inch
slices

8 to 10 white mushrooms,
thickly sliced

4 to 6 plum tomatoes,
halved

½ cup extra virgin olive oil

2 teaspoons sherry vinegar

1½ teaspoons coarse sea
salt

Didier Oudill was among the first Parisian chefs to grill his meats, fish, and vegetables à la plancha—*on a super-hot griddle. Because he first introduced his* parrilladas, *Spanish for mixed grills, at the Café de Paris in the French Basque resort town of Biarritz, diners at Le Dauphin, his Paris bistro, often assume they are French Basque specialties, but it is a cooking technique that he imported from Spain. The inspiration for their composition, though, is closer to home, as in this one made with* tous les légumes du marché, *"all the market vegetables." Feel free to use some or all of the vegetables suggested and to substitute others (red or green peppers, red onions, parboiled cauliflower, portobello mushrooms).*

1. Place the potato slices in boiling water and boil until tender but not yet soft, 13 to 15 minutes. Drain, plunge into ice water, drain, and pat dry.

2. Place the carrots in boiling water and boil until crisp-tender, 7 to 8 minutes. Drain, plunge into ice water, drain, and pat dry.

3. Place the asparagus in boiling water and boil until crisp-tender, 4 to 5 minutes. Drain, plunge into ice water, drain, and pat dry.

4. Preheat the oven to 200°F. Thoroughly rub the bottom of an oven-safe serving platter or baking dish with the cut garlic and place on the oven's middle shelf.

5. Heat a large nonstick skillet over high heat until very hot. Season the potato slices liberally with thyme, salt, and pepper, place in the pan, and cook, turning once, until partly browned, 3 to 4 minutes

per side. Transfer to a corner of the serving platter in the oven to keep warm. Repeat with all the vegetables. Arrange the partly browned vegetables side by side on the serving platter to maintain clear lines of separation among the various colors.

6. Drizzle the *parrillada* vegetables with olive oil, sprinkle with sherry vinegar and coarse sea salt, and serve immediately with Tomato Toast (page 33) or toasted slices of baguette.

Vegetables and Side Dishes

❃

ACCOMPAGNEMENTS

PROVENÇAL TOMATOES *with* THYME

⊙ TOMATES À LA PROVENÇALE, THYM FUMANT ⊙

MAKES 4 SERVINGS

4 firm ripe medium
  tomatoes

Salt

Freshly ground black pepper

2 garlic cloves, chopped

2 tablespoons chopped fresh
  parsley

2 tablespoons bread crumbs

2 tablespoons olive oil

8 sprigs dried thyme
  (see headnote)

Turning every plate into an event is an ideal of high brasserie style. The spellbinding scent emitted by a smoking sprig of dried thyme burned like incense turns Le Grand Colbert's platter of Grilled Lamb Steaks (page 116) into a head-turning seduction, and will accomplish the same for any other meat, chicken, or fish dish you choose to serve these Provençal-style tomatoes with. To dry fresh thyme sprigs, tie them together with a twist tie and hang them upside down in a warm, dry, airy, dark location for 5 to 10 days.

1. Preheat the oven to 375°F. Halve the tomatoes lengthwise, carefully remove the seeds with a teaspoon, sprinkle the cut sides with salt, and turn them upside down on a rack for 15 minutes to drain. Transfer them to a lightly oiled baking pan, cut sides up, and season with pepper.

2. Combine the chopped garlic, parsley, and bread crumbs, spoon this mixture into the tomato cups, sprinkle with olive oil, and bake until the tomatoes are tender and the topping is lightly browned, 15 to 20 minutes.

3. To serve, stick a thyme sprig into each tomato half and light its top with a long match. Serve immediately.

COCOTTE OF SPRING VEGETABLES *with* OLIVE OIL, THYME, *and* ROSEMARY

◦ COCOTTE DE LÉGUMES DE PRINTEMPS À L'HUILE D'OLIVE, THYM, ET ROMARIN ◦

MAKES 6 SIDE-DISH SERVINGS OR 4 MAIN-COURSE SERVINGS

1 pound baby carrots, peeled, or substitute 2 to 3 large carrots, cut into 3-inch sticks

⅓ pound haricots verts or slender green beans, ends clipped

1 fennel bulb, cut into ½-inch wedges

½ pound asparagus, tough stalk ends trimmed

1 cup shelled fresh peas

2 tablespoons unsalted butter

2 tablespoons olive oil

2 tablespoons chopped shallots

4 ounces bacon, diced

2 teaspoons chopped fresh thyme

2 teaspoons chopped fresh rosemary

Salt

Freshly ground black pepper

2 teaspoons chopped chives

Cocotte *refers both to Stéphane Jégo's spring vegetable medley and the cast-iron (casserole) in which it is served. But the suggestion in appellation as well as presentation of long, slow stewing is a clever bistro chef's ruse. That this cocotte's vegetables are cooked only until they are crisp-tender—crunchy, even—reflects the new gospel in bistro cooking: Show each and every ingredient to its best advantage. As such, the repudiation of mushy asparagus and cooked-to-death carrots is not enough. Jégo and several of his contemporaries insist on boiling each vegetable in separate pots of boiling water to preserve their color, taste, and character. Much as I find that almost unnecessary, I do suggest you boil the carrots separately from the green vegetables to preserve the color of each. Serve with meats, fish, or chicken. If preparing as a main course, serve over cooked rice.*

1. Cook the vegetables in boiling salted water until slightly tender, about 3 minutes for the carrots, haricots verts, and fennel; 4 to 5 minutes for the asparagus and peas. Plunge the vegetables into ice water to stop the cooking process and set in the color. Drain and set aside.

2. Heat the butter and olive oil in a casserole or large saucepan over medium heat, add the shallots and bacon and sweat, stirring occasionally, until the shallots are soft and practically melt into the butter and olive oil, about 5 minutes. Add the parboiled vegetables, thyme, and rosemary, season with salt and pepper, and cook, tossing frequently, until the vegetables are hot and crisp-tender, 5 to 7 minutes. Add the chives for the final 30 seconds, mixing well, and serve.

SAUTÉED SPINACH *with* PARMIGIANO-REGGIANO CHIPS

◦ ÉPINARD À CRU, CROUSTILLANT PARMIGIANO-REGGIANO ◦

MAKES 4 SIDE-DISH
SERVINGS

1 1/4 pounds fresh spinach

*1/2 cup finely grated
  Parmigiano-Reggiano*

2 tablespoons butter

Salt

Fresly ground black pepper

Rather than topping his bistro's spinach with grated cheese, Alain Cirelli serves it with crisp, delectable, and easy-to-prepare Parmigiano-Reggiano chips.

1. Trim the large stems from the spinach. Wash and drain the leaves and pat or spin them dry.

2. Heat a large nonstick skillet over medium heat until hot. Sprinkle the grated cheese over the skillet to form 4 mounds at least 2 inches apart. Pat down each mound with the back of a spoon, spreading it to a thin round 3 to 4 inches in diameter. Heat until the cheese melts, bubbles, and finally turns golden brown on the bottom and around the edges, 3 to 4 minutes. Turn carefully with a thin spatula and cook until the other side turns golden, 1 to 2 minutes. Once removed from the heat, the limp chips will quickly harden to a crisp.

3. Melt the butter in a large saucepan over medium heat, add the spinach, season with salt and pepper, and cook, tossing frequently, until wilted, about 1 minute. Remove with a slotted spoon and divide into 4 portions, topping each with a Parmigiano-Reggiano chip.

CELERY ROOT PUREE

○ PURÉE DE CÉLERI-RAVE ○

MAKES 3 TO 6 SIDE-DISH
SERVINGS

1 celery root (about 1½
  pounds), peeled, trimmed,
  and cut into 1-inch cubes

1 quart whole milk

Coarse sea salt

2 tablespoons long-grain
  white rice

¾ cup heavy cream

*Served at Le Beurre Noisette as an accompaniment to the bistro's
rosemary veal roast (page 111), this celery root puree complements
any number of meat, poultry, and fish dishes. For optimum
creaminess, Thierry Blanqui uses rice as the starch in his puree, not
potatoes, the dish's customary thickening agent. The water contained
in the potatoes can dilute the puree's texture as well as its mild taste.
The only risk in preparing it Blanqui's way is that the silky smooth
puree becomes a distraction. You just can't keep your fork away from
it. A quantity that should feed up to six people easily gets polished off
by three.*

1. Place the celery root in a saucepan, cover with the milk, season
with a pinch of salt, and heat over medium-high heat to a boil. Add
the rice, lower the heat to low, partially cover, and simmer, stirring
occasionally, until very soft, 40 to 45 minutes.

2. Drain the celery and rice, reserving the liquid (which, once
cooled, can be frozen and later served as a soup), transfer to a
blender or food processor and puree, scraping down the sides as
necessary, until smooth.

3. Place the cream in a saucepan over medium heat and heat just to
a boil, stirring with a wooden spoon to keep it from boiling over. Reduce the heat to low and simmer until the cream is slightly reduced
and thickened, about 3 minutes. Add the pureed celery root and rice
and cook, stirring constantly, until all the moisture has been absorbed, 2 to 3 minutes. Remove from the heat, season with salt,
whip with a whisk to fluff the puree, and serve.

PARSNIP GRATIN

◦ GRATIN DE PANAIS BOULANGÈRE ◦

MAKES 6 SERVINGS

2 pounds parsnips

2 cups milk

2 cups heavy cream

2 sprigs fresh thyme

2 sprigs fresh rosemary

2 bay leaves

4 to 5 garlic cloves, chopped

Salt

Freshly ground black pepper

1/4 cup grated Parmigiano-
   Reggiano

2 tablespoons butter, cut
   into 1/4-inch cubes, plus
   butter for greasing the pan

Since foraging foreign lands for new ideas is already old hat, bistro chefs like L'Ami Jean's Stéphane Jégo are digging into the past for inspiration. They're reviving subterranean vegetables sworn off by an older generation forced to eat them due to World War II rations and subsequently misunderstood by French baby boomers oblivious to their, well, roots. Paris is going gaga for rutabaga and getting all choked up by the Jerusalem artichoke (page 134). The turnip is turning heads. And the parsnip, though démodé since the Middle Ages, is so hot it merits the sort of treatment rarely afforded even the beloved potato. For this gratin, Jégo bathes and very nearly melts rounds of parsnip measuring .0917 inch—the thickness, he advises, of a 1-euro coin—in a hot, milky bath infused with fresh herbs and garlic. Do not be put off by the high quantity of cream in the poaching liquid. Most is left behind and, endowed with the fashionably sweet, nutty flavor of parsnip, may be saved and recycled as either a sauce for fish, poultry, and vegetables or, mixed with chicken or vegetable stock, a cream of parsnip soup.

1. Peel the parsnips and slice them into rounds about 1/8 inch thick. Set aside.

2. Combine the milk, cream, thyme, rosemary, bay leaves, and garlic in a saucepan, season with salt and pepper, and bring to a boil over high heat. When the liquid begins to foam and rise, quickly lower the heat to low, add the parsnips, and simmer, stirring occasionally, until tender, 35 to 45 minutes.

3. Preheat the broiler and butter a 2-quart gratin dish (or 6 small ones). Remove the parsnips from the cooking liquid with a slotted spoon and arrange them in even layers in the prepared gratin dish.

Pour the cooking liquid through a fine sieve. Spoon ¼ cup of the strained cooking liquid (reserving the remainder, see headnote) over the parsnips, sprinkle with an even layer of cheese, top with the butter cubes, set under the broiler, and cook until golden brown, about 3 minutes.

Dining elbow-to-elbow and hand-to-hand at L'Ami Jean.

GRATIN OF JERUSALEM ARTICHOKES *and* PARSLEY

◦ PERSILLÉ DE TOPINAMBOUR ◦

MAKES 4 SERVINGS

6 tablespoons unsalted butter, cut into small cubes, plus butter for the baking pan

2 pounds Jerusalem artichokes

Pinch of coarse sea salt

1/4 cup chopped flat-leaf parsley

1/4 cup bread crumbs

This gratin showcases the sweet, nutty flavor of Jerusalem artichokes, sometimes esteemed for their crunchiness, in a melted state of utter silkiness. Bruno Doucet serves it at his bistro as a cushion for slices of pan-grilled sirloin. You can do the same by following the directions for Pan-Grilled Rib Steak with Béarnaise Sauce on page 100, substituting sirloin for the rib steak.

1. Preheat the oven to 350°F and generously butter a 10-inch gratin dish or baking dish. Trim the Jerusalem artichokes of any knobs, peel them with a vegetable peeler, and cook them in boiling salted water until tender, 12 to 15 minutes. Drain and, once cool enough to handle, cut into 1/2-inch slices.

2. Layer the Jerusalem artichoke slices, one slightly overlapping the other, on the bottom of the prepared dish, dot with the butter cubes, and sprinkle with the salt, parsley, and bread crumbs. Bake just until lightly golden on top, 15 to 20 minutes. Remove from the oven and let settle a few minutes before serving.

POTATO "MATAFAN"

◦ MATEFAIM ◦

MAKES 4 SERVINGS (8 TO 10 CAKES)

1½ pounds Yukon gold or Idaho russet potatoes

Coarse sea salt

2 egg whites

3 whole eggs, beaten

3 tablespoons heavy cream

½ cup flour

Salt

Freshly ground white or black pepper

Butter

These potato cakes live up to their name: Matafan *and, alternatively,* matefaim *both derive from* mate la faim—*"quell hunger." They are often prepared as a large, single cake; the bistro Aux Lyonnais pairs smaller ones with its chicken in cream sauce (page 97).*

1. Preheat the oven to 400°F. Wash and pat dry the unpeeled potatoes. Sprinkle 2 to 3 tablespoons coarse sea salt on a baking sheet or in a pan to form a bed for the potatoes and bake them until tender, about 1 hour.

2. In a bowl, beat the egg whites with an electric mixer until soft peaks form.

3. When cool enough to handle, halve the potatoes, scoop out the flesh into a mixing bowl, add the whipped egg whites, whole eggs, cream, and flour, season with salt and pepper, and mix well until fully blended.

4. Spoon about 2 tablespoons for each pancake on a buttered baking sheet or pan, flatten each with a spatula, and cook, turning once, until cooked through, 2 minutes on each side.

BERNY POTATOES

◦ POMMES BERNY ◦

MAKES 4 SERVINGS
(ABOUT 1 DOZEN
CROQUETTES)

1½ pounds potatoes,
preferably Yukon gold or
Idaho russet

Salt

3 tablespoons unsalted
butter

3 egg yolks, beaten

1 tablespoon chopped black
truffles or substitute
½ ounce dried porcini
mushrooms and
½ teaspoon truffle oil

Flour

½ cup finely slivered
almonds

Vegetable oil, for frying

*At this brasserie and elsewhere, Berny potatoes are fluffy almond
and potato croquettes containing the heady perfume of black truffles.
As a substitute for black truffles, I use dried porcini mushrooms and
truffle oil. Even without the truffle flavor they are first-rate croquettes.*

1. Preheat the oven to 400°F. Peel and wash the potatoes, cut them
into 1-inch cubes, place them in a saucepan, cover with water, season with salt, and heat over high heat to a boil. Continue to cook,
regulating the heat so the water does not boil over, until the potatoes are tender, about 20 minutes. Drain.

2. Transfer the potatoes to a baking dish, and bake until they are
thoroughly dried out, about 10 minutes.

3. Puree the potatoes through a food mill or mash with a potato
masher. Transfer to a mixing bowl, add the butter, and mix well.
Slowly add the egg yolks, mixing continuously until fully incorporated. Stir in the chopped truffles. (If using porcini mushrooms,
pour boiling water over them and let soak for 20 minutes. Drain and
chop the porcini and add to the potato mixture.)

4. Coating your hands lightly with flour, roll the potato mixture to
the size of golf balls and flatten each a little to form 1-inch-thick
patties. Dredge each ball in the slivered almonds to coat on both
sides.

5. Heat ½ inch of oil in a large, heavy-bottomed saucepan over
moderately high heat and fry the potato patties, turning once, until
golden brown on both sides, about 3 minutes. Drain on paper
towels and serve.

FRENCH FRIES

MAKES 4 SERVINGS

2 pounds Idaho russet potatoes, peeled and thoroughly dried

Peanut oil

Salt

To give your frites *the deep golden base color and glistening bronze highlights of Le Bistrot Paul Bert's beauties, keep moisture to an absolute minimum. Do not wash or soak the cut potatoes and be sure to dry them thoroughly. It is essential that you fry them twice in small batches, at low and then high temperatures as they do at the Paul Bert. To that end, chef Thierry Laurent uses a deep sauté pan as opposed to a deep fryer. Finally, do not strive for machine-like perfection in the sizing of your* frites. *They should look hand cut, with no two* frites *exactly alike.*

1. Hand cut the potatoes into strips approximately ¾ inch wide and ⅓ inch thick.

2. Clip a deep-frying thermometer to the side of a deep, heavy-bottomed saucepan. Heat 3 inches of peanut oil over moderately high heat to between 320° and 325°F. Place a third of the potatoes in the oil and blanch them, keeping an eye on the temperature and adjusting the heat accordingly, just until they stiffen some and barely begin to color, 6 to 7 minutes. Remove the potatoes with a frying basket, metal strainer, or slotted spoon, drain on paper towels, and set aside for up to 2 hours at room temperature. Repeat with second and third batches. Do not discard the oil.

3. Just before serving, heat the same oil to 360 or 370°F and working this time in two batches, fry the potatoes until deep golden brown, 2 to 3 minutes. Remove the *frites* with a slotted spoon, drain on paper towels, sprinkle with salt, and serve immediately with Béarnaise Sauce (page 101), mayonnaise (page 31), Dijon mustard, ketchup, vinegar, or with steak (page 100).

PIPÉRADE

MAKES 4 SERVINGS

1 red pepper

1 green pepper

2 tomatoes, peeled and seeds
   removed

4 tablespoons olive oil

2 onions, chopped

1 garlic clove, crushed

Pinch of piment d'Espelette
   or cayenne

2 large eggs, beaten

Salt

Freshly ground black pepper

1 tablespoon chopped flat-
   leaf parsley

A classic from France's Basque country, pipérade *can be many things to many people: sauce, dip, garnish, filling, side dish, egg accompaniment, departure point for dishes both traditional and contemporary, simple and complex. At the Bistrot des Capucins, the* pipérade *cushions its ham-wrapped salt cod (page 94). By doubling the quantity of eggs, you can serve it as a main course at breakfast, lunch, or brunch.*

1. Preheat the broiler to high. Place the red and green peppers in a shallow roasting pan and broil about 3 inches from the heat, turning occasionally with tongs, until the skins are blackened. Transfer the peppers to a plastic bag, twist it tightly shut, and let stand for 15 minutes. When cool enough to handle, pull off the charred skin with your fingers. Cut the peppers into ⅓-inch strips, discarding the seeds and pulpy inner core.

2. Cut a small X in the smooth ends of the tomatoes and plunge into boiling salted water for 30 seconds. Drain them and, once cool enough to handle, peel and chop them, discarding the peel and seeds.

3. Heat the olive oil in a saucepan over low heat, add the onions and cook, stirring occasionally, until they are soft but not browned, about 15 minutes.

4. Add the chopped tomatoes, roasted pepper strips, garlic, and piment d'Espelette and cook over a very low flame, stirring occasionally, until the tomato juice is evaporated and the vegetables have softened and melted together, about 15 minutes.

5. Gently stir in the eggs, cover, and cook until the eggs are set, 2 to 3 minutes. Season with salt and pepper, garnish with parsley, and serve.

INDIAN-STYLE VEGETABLE PICKLES

◦ ACHARDS AUX LÉGUMES ◦

MAKES 4 TO 6 SERVINGS

½ pound haricots verts or slender green beans, trimmed and halved

1 cup red wine vinegar

2 cups olive oil

1 small orange, washed and quartered

1 lemon, washed and quartered

½ teaspoon chopped fresh ginger

1 teaspoon curry powder

½ teaspoon paprika

¼ to ½ teaspoon cayenne pepper

1 large carrot, peeled and cut into 2-inch sticks

1 cup cauliflower florets

Salt

Achards (achars) are strongly spiced pickles made from fruits and vegetables. They play a central role in Indian cuisine and are popular as a condiment and hors d'oeuvre in the French Creole cooking of Africa and the West Indies. La Coupole serves a mildly spiced mix of carrot, cauliflower, and haricot vert achards *at room temperature in a small ramekin as an accompaniment for its signature lamb curry (page 114).*

1. Cook the haricots verts in boiling salted water for 5 minutes. Drain, plunge into cold water, drain again, and pat dry.

2. Combine the vinegar and olive oil in a saucepan and heat over high heat to a boil. Add the orange quarters, lemon quarters, ginger, curry, paprika, and cayenne and return to a boil. Add the carrot and cauliflower, lower the heat, and simmer for 45 minutes. Add the haricots verts and cook for an additional 15 minutes. Remove from the heat and let cool. Season with salt, transfer to a lidded jar or other airtight container, and let marinate for 2 days before serving.

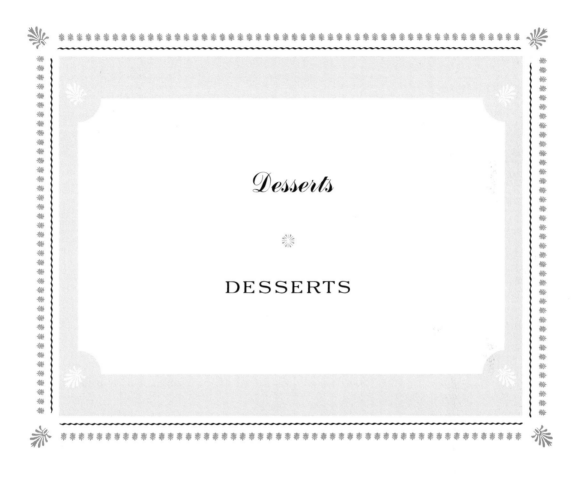

Desserts

DESSERTS

RED BERRY GAZPACHO

◦ GASPACHO DES FRUITS ROUGES ◦

MAKES 4 SERVINGS

1 cup fresh basil leaves

1 quart strawberries, stems removed

2 cups raspberries

½ cup red currants

3 to 4 thin slices pain d'épice, toasted (see headnote)

Juice of 1 lemon (3 tablespoons)

½ cup confectioners' sugar

This isn't just a fancy name for a chilled fruit soup. The addition of toasted pain d'épice *(gingerbread) but no water gives it a thick, almost grainy texture comparable to a pureed tomato gazpacho. The basil provides a Mediterranean nuance. If you don't have access to* pain d'épice *or gingerbread, replace it with slices of white toast and tiny pinches of ground cinnamon, ground cloves, and ground ginger or six gingersnap cookies, reducing the quantity of confectioners' sugar by a tablespoon.*

1. Place the basil leaves in a food processor and process until finely chopped.

2. Chop 1 cup strawberries and set aside. Set aside ½ cup raspberries. Place the remaining ingredients in the food processor with the chopped basil and process until smooth, about 30 seconds. Refrigerate for at least 2 hours.

3. To serve, place some of the chopped strawberries and reserved raspberries on the bottom of four soup bowls and ladle the berry soup on top.

TROPICAL FRUIT SOUP

◦ SOUPE FROIDE DE FRUITS EXOTIQUES ◦

MAKES 4 SERVINGS

1 cup dry white wine

¾ cup honey

1 ripe papaya, peeled and chopped

1 ripe mango, peeled and chopped

2 kiwis, peeled

½ cup passion fruit pulp

¾ cup pineapple chunks, fresh or canned

3 to 4 ounces dark chocolate pastilles or chocolate, broken into small squares

This is but one part of this bistro's deluxe dessert trio, also featuring a Roast Mango Compote with Parsley Sorbet (page 146) and Pineapple Brochettes with Saffron Caramel (page 147). You can certainly prepare the three together, but I suggest serving them separately as stand-alone desserts.

1. Combine the wine and honey and heat to a boil. Place this mixture and all the fruit in a blender and puree until smooth. Chill for 2 hours before serving.

2. Serve chilled with dark chocolate pastilles (or pieces of your favorite chocolate) atop the soup.

ROAST MANGO COMPOTE
with PARSLEY SORBET

◦ COMPOTE DE MANGUES RÔTIES AU FOUR, SORBET DE PERSIL PLATS ◦

MAKES 4 SERVINGS

3 ripe mangoes, peeled and
  cut into chunks

1½ cups sugar

3 tablespoons freshly
  squeezed lemon juice

1 bunch flat-leaf parsley

The sorbet makes this a remarkably light, fragrant, and refreshing summer dessert; its cool, sweet parsley flavor is a revelation.

1. Preheat the oven to 350°F. Place the mango chunks in a baking dish and bake until soft but not yet colored, 35 to 45 minutes.

2. Meanwhile, prepare the sorbet: Combine the sugar, lemon juice, and 2 cups water and heat to a boil. Remove from the heat, submerge the parsley in the liquid, and let steep for 15 minutes. Pass the liquid through a fine sieve into a stainless-steel bowl and freeze for 1 hour. Beat the mixture with a whisk. If preparing with an ice cream maker, freeze the mixture according to the manufacturer's directions. If not, return the mixture to the freezer and beat every 30 minutes or so until frozen, 2 to 3 hours.

3. Transfer the roast mango to a blender and puree until smooth. Let cool and refrigerate.

4. Serve the mango compote chilled with scoops of the parsley sorbet.

PINEAPPLE BROCHETTES
with SAFFRON CARAMEL

◦ BROCHETTES D'ANANAS AU CARAMEL SAFRANÉ ◦

MAKES 4 SERVINGS

1 pineapple

¼ cup granulated sugar

½ teaspoon powdered saffron

When chewing the warm pineapple chunks that slide off these brochettes, a little of the saffron-scented caramel will invariably get caught in your teeth. But it is the sweet, perfumed intensity resulting through caramelization that will stay with you forever. Adding sugar and spice augment the true pineapple flavor to create an indelible dessert sensation.

1. Peel and slice the pineapple into rounds ¾ inch in thickness. Cut the core out of each with a knife or a small cookie cutter. Cut the pineapple slices into ¾-inch cubes. Thread the cubes onto 8 wood skewers.

2. Place the sugar in a saucepan large enough to hold the skewers flat in one layer over low heat and heat until melted. Stir in the saffron with a wooden spoon and raise the heat to medium-high. Place the skewers in the melted sugar and cook, turning often, until the syrup turns a deep caramel color and the pineapple chunks are lightly caramelized on all sides, about 10 minutes. Remove from the heat (be careful, they're hot) and serve.

LIME CUSTARD *with* ORANGE TUILE

◦ CRÉMEUX DE CITRON VERT, TUILE À L'ORANGE ◦

MAKES 6 SERVINGS

1 teaspoon unflavored
  gelatin

1 cup heavy cream

2 eggs, beaten

⅓ cup sugar

1 cup freshly squeezed lime
  juice

4 tablespoons unsalted
  butter, cut into small pieces

6 Orange Tuiles (recipe
  follows)

True to its name, this bistro's crémeux, *meaning something creamy, is creamier and more custardy than a* panna cotta *or a* flan, *yet not as rich as a mousse. Its smoothness is contrasted by the crispness of an orange* tuile *(or tile cookie). This particular* tuile *is a flat, wafer-thin disk, rather than the typically curved shape that gives it its name (*tuile *is French for "tile"), and, for extra delicacy, is made without the ground nuts that give other* tuiles *their crunch. Stéphane Danière also serves a passion fruit* crémeux, *which can be prepared by substituting one cup of passion fruit puree for the lime juice.*

1. Pour 2 tablespoons cold water into a cup, sprinkle the gelatin over it, and let stand until softened, about 5 minutes.

2. Heat the cream in a saucepan over medium heat until it steams but does not boil.

3. Combine the eggs and sugar in a mixing bowl and whisk until the sugar is dissolved and the mixture is thick and foamy. Transfer the mixture into a heavy saucepan and heat over medium-low heat, whisking continuously, until thick and pale yellow. Add the lime juice and whisk until well blended.

4. Stir in the gelatin mixture, add the cream and beat with a whisk until well blended, and remove from the heat. Add the butter, one piece at a time, beating continuously with a whisk until each piece is dissolved before adding the next one.

5. Pour the mixture into six custard cups or ramekins and set aside to cool for 15 minutes. Refrigerate until set, at least 4 hours. Place an orange tuile atop each serving.

ORANGE TUILES
(tuiles à l'orange)

....

MAKES 12 TO 16 TUILES

½ cup granulated sugar

¼ cup brown sugar

½ cup flour

6 tablespoons unsalted butter, softened at room temperature, plus butter for the cookie sheet

½ cup freshly squeezed orange juice

1 teaspoon grated orange zest

1. Preheat the oven to 350°F. Sift the granulated sugar, brown sugar, and flour into a mixing bowl and mix well. Add the butter, little by little, beating the mixture with the whisk attachment of an electric mixer, until fully incorporated and smooth. Add the orange juice and orange zest and beat until fully incorporated.

2. Working in small batches, drop a heaping teaspoon of the batter onto a greased nonstick cookie sheet and use the back of a spoon dipped in cold milk to gently flatten each mound of batter into an extremely thin round 3½ to 4 inches in diameter. Repeat, spacing the rounds at least 3 inches apart, to form as many *tuiles* as will fit on the sheet. Bake the *tuiles* until they are golden brown, 7 to 9 minutes. Remove the *tuiles* from the oven and let them cool for 2 minutes. Using a thin spatula, delicately lift up the *tuiles* from the cookie sheet and transfer them to a plate. Repeat until all the batter has been used. Store unused *tuiles* in a plastic bag or cookie jar.

PANNA COTTA *with* RASPBERRY PRESERVES

◦ PANNA COTTA À LA VANILLE, CONFITURE DE FRAMBOISES ◦

MAKES 4 SERVINGS

1 teaspoon unflavored
  gelatin

2 cups light cream

½ vanilla bean or 1¼
  teaspoons pure vanilla
  extract

¼ cup sugar

8 ounces raspberry preserves

1 cup fresh raspberries

Chef Bruno Doucet gives this Italian dessert a bistro spin by layering the chilled custard like a fine pastry between raspberry preserves and fresh raspberries.

1. Pour 2 tablespoons cold water into a cup, sprinkle the gelatin over it, and let stand until softened, about 5 minutes.

2. Pour the cream into a saucepan. Split the vanilla bean half in two lengthwise and scrape the seeds into the cream. Add the vanilla pod and sugar, turn the heat to medium, and cook until the cream steams but does not boil. Remove from the heat, add the gelatin mixture, and stir until dissolved. Strain the mixture through a fine sieve into a bowl and let cool for 20 minutes.

3. Spoon a quarter of the raspberry preserves on the bottom of four custard cups or ramekins to form a smooth layer, pour the cream mixture over the preserves, and refrigerate until set, at least 5 hours.

4. To serve, top each with a layer of fresh raspberries.

CRÈME CARAMEL

MAKES 6 TO 8 SERVINGS

3½ cups sugar

3 cups milk

2 teaspoons pure vanilla extract

7 eggs

If there exists an interpretation of crème caramel superior to Joël Fleury's, I'd rather not know about it. Limiting myself to a single adult portion of his silky version, daringly presented at this brasserie in a large terrine from which diners help themselves, is already a hopeless endeavor. The suggestion of a smoother, creamier, more irresistible flan, however unlikely, is itself too dangerously tantalizing to entertain.

1. To make the caramel, combine 1 cup sugar and ½ cup water in a heavy-bottomed saucepan over moderate heat and stir until the sugar is dissolved. Continue to cook the syrup, swirling it and tilting the pan and scraping down the sides, until it turns a deep golden color, 8 to 10 minutes. Pour the caramel into a loaf pan (or deep baking dish) and quickly turn and tilt the pan so that the caramel covers the entire bottom in an even layer. Set aside.

2. Preheat the oven to 300°F. Combine the milk and vanilla in a saucepan over medium heat and heat through but do not boil. Remove from the heat and cover to keep warm.

3. Combine the remaining 2½ cups sugar and the eggs in a mixing bowl and beat with a whisk until pale and foamy, about 5 minutes. Continue to whisk while slowly pouring the hot milk, little by little, over the eggs and beat until the mixture is homogeneous in color. Pour this mixture into the loaf pan over the caramel.

4. Make a bain-marie by placing the loaf pan in a larger pan and filling the outer pan with enough hot water to reach about halfway up the side of the loaf pan. Place the pans in the oven and bake for 50 minutes, or until a knife blade inserted in the center comes out clean. Remove from the oven and let cool on a wire rack for 1 hour.

Cover with plastic wrap and refrigerate for at least 2 hours and up to 2 days.

5. To serve, carefully run a sharp knife around the inside of the pan to loosen the flan. Bring the pan to the table and serve as you would a terrine, cutting thick slices and spooning caramel over and around each serving of the flan.

WARM ALMOND CAKE
with CARAMEL CREAM

◦ GÂTEAU MOELLEUX AMANDINE, CONFITURE DE LAIT À LA CRÈME ◦

MAKES 6 SERVINGS

7 tablespoons butter, melted, plus butter for the pan

½ cup flour, plus flour for the ramekins

1 cup Milk Caramel (recipe follows) or dulce de leche, jarred or homemade

½ cup light cream

½ cup blanched almonds

½ cup plus 2 tablespoons sugar

5 eggs

The objective that inspired Rodolphe Paquin's warm, caramel-gushing almond cakes is one likely shared by many an overburdened, over-chocolated dinner host. With too little time and space at his bistro to contemplate elaborate, prepared-to-order pastries, he sought to create a dessert that could be served hot and fast and wasn't chocolate. He mixes, molds, and freezes his cakes in advance and then bakes them to order, requiring that diners wait twelve excruciatingly long minutes for delivery. Their creamy, oozy interior is the result not of deliberate undercooking, the core technique of most molten chocolate cakes, but rather of spooning caramel cream into the just-baked gâteau. The filling, a blend of cream and confiture de lait, *France's equivalent of Argentina's dulce de leche, is warmed by the hot cake as it travels from kitchen to dining room. While Paquin uses pastry rings to shape his cakes, you can use a jumbo muffin pan, as instructed here, or individual ramekins. The milk caramel may also be deployed as a filling for Dessert Crêpes (page 185), a topping for ice cream and pastries, or a toasted bread spread akin to Nutella or peanut butter.*

1. Preheat the oven to 400°F and generously butter and flour a 6-cup jumbo-sized muffin pan (or six 1-cup ramekins), tapping out any excess flour.

2. Combine the milk caramel and light cream in a mixing bowl and mix well with a metal spoon until fully blended. (If the milk caramel is too solid to work with, soften it by warming it either in the microwave or in a glass jar set in hot water reaching two-thirds up its sides.) Set the caramel cream aside.

3. Place the almonds and 1 tablespoon sugar in a food processor fitted with the metal blade and grind just until they turn into a granular powder, 30 to 40 seconds.

4. Combine the eggs and the remaining sugar in a double boiler over low to medium heat (the water should be hot but not boiling) and beat with a whisk until pale and thick, about 10 minutes. Add the flour and ground almond powder and mix well. Add the melted butter and mix until fully incorporated.

5. Spoon the cake batter into the cups until two-thirds full. Bake until golden brown and mostly cooked through but still moist in the center, 10 to 11 minutes. Not waiting for the cakes to cool, carefully run a thin sharp knife between the cakes and the pan and unmold them onto six plates. Working quickly, one cake at a time, use the stem of a spoon to pierce a small hole about 1 inch deep into the middle of each cake and spoon caramel cream into the hole and over the top of the cake. Serve immediately.

MILK CARAMEL
(confiture de lait)

MAKES ABOUT 1 CUP

2 cups whole milk

1 cup sugar

2 teaspoons pure vanilla extract

¼ teaspoon baking soda

1. Combine all the ingredients in a saucepan and heat over medium heat just to a boil. Lower the heat to medium low and cook, stirring frequently with a wooden spoon, until the mixture turns a caramel color and thickens enough that the bottom of the pan is visible while the sauce is being stirred, about 60 minutes. Remove from the heat and let cool. Transfer to a lidded jar or other airtight container and store in the refrigerator.

2. To soften the milk caramel before using, warm it in the microwave or submerge the jar in hot water reaching two-thirds up its sides.

BABA AU RHUM

MAKES 6 TO 8 SERVINGS

1 cup golden raisins

½ to 1 cup dark rum

6 tablespoons unsalted
butter, plus butter for the
pan

1 envelope (2½ teaspoons)
active dry yeast

1½ cups flour

¼ teaspoon salt

4 eggs

1 cup plus 2 tablespoons
sugar

2 cups whipped cream,
optional

A sweetened bread cake drenched with rum syrup, this brasserie classic is thought to have been the royal brainchild of Stanislaus Leszczynski (1677–1766). During his exile in Alsace and Lorraine, the deposed king of Poland complained that kouglof, the region's popular yeast bread (page 181), was dry, and suggested it be doused with something alcoholic. He was reading 1001 Arabian Nights *at the time and named the confection he inspired Ali Baba. When his daughter Marie married Louis XV in 1725, she took her father's pastry chef, Nicolas Stohrer, and his rum syrup–soaked kouglof with her to Versailles. Five years later Stohrer opened his eponymous pastry shop on the rue Montorgueil in Paris (which to this day counts the baba among its signature cakes). The success of baba au rhum in the French capital made it a natural choice for the Alsatian owners of the late-nineteenth- and early-twentieth-century brasseries, who traced the cake's route to Paris from northeastern France.*

Balzar's excellent baba differs from the many versions in two important respects: First, it's baked in a long rectangular mold and not one that is cylindrical or, in the manner of a savarin, ring-shaped. Second, the rum is left out of the syrup and instead served in a bottle at the table, leaving the dosage to the diner's discretion or lack thereof. If you'd prefer to prepare yours presoaked in rum, simply add the rum drained from the raisins to the sugar and water immediately before heating the syrup in step 5.

1. Sprinkle the raisins with ½ cup rum and let macerate for up to a day.

2. Cut the butter into cubes and let soften at room temperature.

3. Dissolve the yeast in 2 tablespoons warm water and let stand for 10 minutes.

4. In a large bowl, combine the flour and salt and make a well in the center. Beat 2 eggs and pour into the well. Add the yeast mixture

and 2 tablespoons sugar and mix with a wooden spoon until the dough has a homogeneous texture. Beat the remaining 2 eggs and gradually add to the dough, mixing the pastry mixture vigorously with a wooden spoon. Add the butter cubes, one by one, and knead with your hands, lifting and pulling the mixture with your fingertips, until the lumps are gone and the dough is smooth and elastic, about 5 minutes. Add the drained raisins (reserving the rum) and mix until evenly distributed. Place the dough as evenly as possible into a buttered 1 to 1½-quart loaf pan, smooth the top, sprinkle with a little flour, cover with a damp towel, and let rise in a warm place until doubled in bulk, about 1 hour.

5. Preheat the oven to 350°F. Bake the baba until golden brown and a knife inserted in the center comes out clean, about 25 minutes.

6. Meanwhile, combine 1 cup sugar and 2 cups water (and rum if desired; see headnote) in a saucepan and heat over moderately high heat to a boil. Remove from the heat and stir with a wooden spoon until the sugar dissolves. Let cool a few minutes.

7. Set a wire rack over a deep dish or tray. Unmold the baba onto the wire rack, centering it over the deep dish, puffed side up, and let cool for 10 minutes. Prick the top of the baba in several places with a fork. Pour about two-thirds of the lukewarm syrup over the baba and let stand for 30 minutes, basting frequently with the remaining syrup as well as the syrup that drains into the deep dish.

8. To serve, cut the drenched baba into slices, drizzle each, according to taste, with rum, and serve with whipped cream, if desired.

BRIE STUFFED *with* MASCARPONE *and* DRIED FRUITS

◦ BRIE FARCI AVEC FRUITS SECS ◦

MAKES 6 TO 8 SERVINGS

1/4 cup mascarpone cheese

1 tablespoon golden raisins

2 dried apricots, chopped

2 prunes, chopped

2 dried figs, chopped

1/2 teaspoon coarse sea salt

One 1-pound round Brie

2 tablespoon sherry vinegar

1/2 teapoon Dijon mustard

1 tablespoon hazelnut oil

3 tablespoons olive oil

Freshly ground black pepper

4 cups mixed salad greens, torn into large bite-size pieces

1/2 cup chopped walnuts

1 French country bread or other crusty bread

One of the drawbacks of moving from the kitchen of a Michelin-starred restaurant to that of a modest bistro is that lower pricing restricts a chef's freedom to play with such extravagances as morels, lobster, caviar, foie gras, and, most of all, black truffles. To help himself and maybe also his budget-conscious diners forget their truffled pasts, Thierry Blanqui styled this rich cheese dessert after Brie au mascarpone truffé (Brie stuffed with shaved truffles and Italian mascarpone cheese), a dessert-cheese creation championed by Alain Dutournier of the two-Michelin-starred Carré des Feuillants in Paris and featured in one form or another at finer restaurants throughout France. For the filling, Blanqui keeps the creamy mascarpone but replaces the costly truffles and their earthiness with several dried fruits, most crucially dried figs. He admits to a second inspiration for introducing this dish: his dislike, dare one say, of Brie. "It's pasty," he says with a wince, voicing an opinion shared by many French but uttered by few.

1. Combine the mascarpone, raisins, apricots, prunes, figs, and salt in a bowl and mix well until the dried fruits are evenly distributed.

2. Halve the Brie round horizontally with a carving knife. Spread the mascarpone mixture evenly over the bottom halves and then re-place the top halves to form a sandwich. Store in the refrigerator for at least 30 minutes and up to 3 days.

3. About 1 hour before serving, remove the stuffed Brie from the refrigerator and slice with a carving knife into 6 or 8 triangular or rectangular wedges. Leave out to soften some at room temperature.

4. Immediately before serving, prepare the vinaigrette: Combine the vinegar and mustard and mix with a whisk. Slowly whisk in the hazelnut oil and olive oil and season with pepper. Toss the salad greens with the vinaigrette and chopped walnuts and divide into 6 or 8 portions. Serve each with a wedge of stuffed Brie and slices of French country bread.

BEIGNETS *with* ORANGE-FLOWER JELLY

◦ PETS DE NONNES, GELÉE FLEUR D'ORANGER ◦

MAKES 35 TO 40 BEIGNETS

3 tablespoons granulated sugar

3 tablespoons unsalted butter

Pinch of salt

½ cup flour

2 eggs

Vegetable oil, for frying

3 to 4 tablespoons confectioners' sugar

Orange-Flower Jelly (recipe follows)

According to legend, a nun at the Benedictine Abbey de Marmoutier in Normandy was fixing dinner when she passed wind amid the other sisters of the convent. Mortified to be the object of their ridicule, she dropped a spoonful of pastry dough into a pot of hot oil. The mishap inspired the beignets that came to be known as pets de nonnes, *"nuns' farts." These warm beignets are served at this bistro like jelly donuts, only the runny orange-flower jelly is kept outside the pastry in the form of a cold dip. Orange-flower water, a natural extract distilled from bitter orange blossoms, is more pungent and perfumed than orange zest. It is sold at Middle Eastern and Indian markets, natural foods stores, and fine liquor stores and may also be purchased from www.thespicehouse.com and www.gourmetsleuth.com.*

1. Combine the sugar, butter, salt, and 1 cup cold water in a saucepan over medium-high heat and bring to a boil, stirring with a wooden spoon so that the melted butter dissolves. Turn off the heat, add all the flour at once, and stir with a wooden spoon, scraping the sides of the saucepan, until fully incorporated. Turn the heat on low and cook, stirring constantly, until the batter dries a little and stops sticking to the pan. Remove the pan from the heat and add the eggs, one at a time, mixing vigorously until each egg is fully incorporated before adding the next.

2. Clip a deep-frying thermometer to a large heavy-bottomed saucepan and heat 2 inches of oil over moderately high heat to 325°F. Working in batches of no more than a dozen beignets, use one teaspoon to gather a rounded spoonful of pastry and another teaspoon to push the pastry into the hot oil. Fry until golden brown, turning the beignets and keeping them apart, until golden brown, about 2 minutes. Drain the beignets on paper towels, sprinkle with confectioners' sugar, and serve with orange-flower jelly.

ORANGE-FLOWER JELLY
(gelée fleur d'oranger)

YIELDS 2 CUPS

*3 tablespoons grated orange
  zest*

½ cup sugar

*One ¼-ounce envelope
  unflavored gelatin*

*1 teaspoon orange-flower
  water or substitute 1
  additional teaspoon grated
  orange zest*

1. Place the orange zest in boiling water and cook for 2 minutes. Drain through a fine sieve, reserving the zest.

2. Pour 2 tablespoons cold water into a cup, sprinkle the gelatin over it, and let stand until softened, about 5 minutes.

3. Combine the sugar, orange zest, orange-flower water, and 2 cups cold water in a saucepan and heat over medium heat, stirring occasionally with a wooden spoon, until the mixture steams but does not boil. Remove from the heat, stir in the gelatin mixture, and let stand for 20 minutes. Refrigerate until the jelly is set, at least 5 hours and up to 4 days.

ORANGE RICE PUDDING

◦ RIZ AU LAIT ET ROSACE D'ORANGES ◦

MAKES 4 SERVINGS

½ cup short-grain rice

Salt

4 oranges

2 cups whole milk

3 tablespoons sugar

2 tablespoons orange
   marmalade

Orange Caramel Sauce
   (recipe follows), optional

The great rice pudding revival taking hold of Paris is an oddly quiet phenomenon. In interviews for this book, individual bistro chefs like Gérard Fouché were genuinely surprised to learn that dozens of their colleagues had also added a riz au lait *to their dessert menus during the last few years. Hankerings for home-style throwbacks are univeral: You will be among many instantly enticed by Fouché's creamy rice pudding. The Orange Caramel Sauce may also be served with the Molten Chocolate Cake (page 176).*

1. Place the rice in a saucepan, cover with cold water and a pinch of salt, and bring to a boil. Remove from the heat and drain.

2. Grate the zest of 1 orange. Peel all the oranges, divide them into sections, and refrigerate until ready to serve.

3. Combine the orange zest, milk, and sugar in a saucepan and heat over high heat to a boil.

4. Add the rice, cover, lower the heat to very low, and cook, stirring occasionally so the rice does not stick, for 30 minutes.

5. Remove the rice from the heat, add the orange marmalade, stir well, and let cool. Refrigerate until ready to serve.

6. To serve, surround each serving of rice pudding with orange sections and drizzle all, if desired, with Orange Caramel Sauce.

ORANGE CARAMEL SAUCE
(sauce caramel à l'orange)

½ cup sugar

2 tablespoons fresh orange juice

2 tablespoons Grand Marnier or other orange liqueur

Combine the sugar and orange juice in a heavy-bottomed saucepan over moderate heat and stir until the sugar is dissolved. Continue to cook the syrup, swirling it and tilting the pan, until it turns a deep golden caramel, 8 to 10 minutes. Remove from the heat and very slowly stir in the Grand Marnier to deglaze the pan and prevent the caramel from quickly hardening. Serve immediately.

POACHED WHITE PEACHES *with* HONEY *and* LEMON VERBENA

◦ PÊCHES BLANCHES POCHÉ AU MIEL ET VERVEINE ◦

MAKES 6 SERVINGS

6 ripe white peaches

¾ cup honey

10 dried lemon verbena leaves

Vanilla ice cream or pound cake, optional

Someday someone will introduce white peaches, honey, and lemon verbena as a new flavor of premium ice cream. At least I hope so. Meanwhile, this bracingly sweet combination from wine bar chef Raquel Carena transforms an easy-to-prepare dessert—poached fruit—into a summer treat of stunning simplicity and refreshment. If you can't get your hands on the lemon verbena leaves, substitute 1 tablespoon lemon juice and ½ teaspoon lemon zest. Though the perfume is quite different, the results are extremely satisfying.

1. Place the peaches in boiling water and boil for 1 minute. Drain them and plunge into ice water. Peel and halve the peaches, remove the pits, and place in a single layer, cut side down, on the bottom of a large bowl or plastic storage container.

2. Combine the honey and ¼ cup water and heat over medium-high heat, stirring occasionally with a wooden spoon, to a boil. Add the lemon verbena leaves, remove from the heat, and let steep for 5 minutes. Pour the syrup and leaves over the peaches, set aside for 2 hours at room temperature, and then refrigerate. Serve the peaches and syrup with vanilla ice cream or pound cake, if desired.

WARM APPLE TART

⸙ TARTE AUX POMMES TIÈDES ⸙

MAKES 4 SERVINGS

4 to 5 Golden Delicious apples, peeled, cored, halved, and sliced ½ inch thick

3 tablespoons freshly squeezed lemon juice

One 17¼-ounce package frozen puff pastry sheets, thawed

Flour, for the work surface

8 tablespoons (1 stick) unsalted butter, cut into small cubes and warmed to room temperature

½ cup sugar

Vanilla ice cream, crème fraîche, or whipped cream, optional

The characteristic that makes bistro chef Didier Oudill's apple tart crusty and rustic is the treatment of what he and others sometimes refer to as its trottoir, *its "sidewalk." To ensure a golden brown periphery of unimpeded puffiness, he advises tracing a plate, saucer, or other round object of the appropriate size with a knife to score a very shallow inner circle about one-half inch from the outer rim of each pastry round. Apples may be placed atop the pastry in any pattern within the border. For an apple walnut tart, sprinkle ¼ cup coarsely chopped walnuts (1 tablespoon per tart) atop the apples only—please, keep those nuts off the sidewalk!*

1. Preheat the oven to 425°F. Place the apples in a bowl, sprinkle with the lemon juice, and toss (this prevents the apples from browning).

2. Roll out two sheets of pastry on a lightly floured work surface to ⅛ inch thick. Cut out four rounds (two rounds per sheet) 6½ to 7 inches in diameter and transfer them to a baking sheet. Use a paring knife to carefully score a very shallow circle about ½ inch inside the outer rim of the dough rounds (see headnote).

3. Arrange the apples atop the dough rounds within the confines of the inner circles in a tight, circular pattern. Scatter half the butter cubes (1 tablespoon per tart) over the apples and again clear of the borders. Sprinkle with half the sugar (about 1 tablespoon per tart) and bake for 15 minutes.

4. Scatter the remaining butter cubes atop the tarts, sprinkle with the remaining sugar, and bake until the tart's rim is a deep golden brown and the apples are golden, 15 to 20 additional minutes. Serve warm with vanilla ice cream, crème fraîche, or whipped cream, or plain.

STRAWBERRY NAPOLEON

° MILLEFEUILLE CRAQUANT AUX FRAISES °

MAKES 4 SERVINGS

1⅓ cups flour

⅓ cup granulated sugar

¾ cup (1½ sticks) unsalted butter

1 cup confectioners' sugar

Pastry Cream (recipe follows)

1 pint fresh strawberries, sliced

1 cup Raspberry Sauce (page 175)

You might choose to layer your strawberry napoleon between four sugar crisps, as bistro chef Laurent Aulard suggests. You might even add a penthouse atop the fourth floor. But I'm convinced that three of those hardened crisps provide all the sweet crunch you could possibly need as you break apart this round tower of pastry cream and strawberries. You can bake the crisps separately and serve them as very sweet cookies.

1. Preheat the oven to 400°F. Line a baking sheet with parchment paper.

2. Combine the flour and granulated sugar in a large bowl and mix well.

3. Heat the butter and confectioners' sugar in a saucepan over medium heat, stirring occasionally with a wooden spoon, until the mixture is smooth and homogeneous. Pour the butter mixture into the flour mixture and mix well until smooth. Form the dough into 12 balls about 1½ inches in diameter (the precise measurement matters less than that the balls are all roughly the same size). Place the balls on the parchment-lined baking sheet at lease 2 inches apart, flatten them with the back of a spoon dipped in cold milk, and then flatten the balls further with your fingers and bake into golden-rimmed disks, 12 to 15 minutes. Place the baking sheet on a cooling rack and let the disks harden to a crisp.

4. Place a single crisp in the center of four dessert plates. Put the pastry cream in a pastry bag and pipe a thin layer of cream over the crisps. Arrange some of the strawberry slices on top of the cream, top each with a second crisp, another layer of cream and strawberries, and then a third disk. Drizzle the raspberry sauce on top and around the napoleons and serve.

PASTRY CREAM
(crème pâtissière)

YIELDS ABOUT 3 CUPS

*½ vanilla bean, split
lengthwise and scraped, or
substitute 1 tablespoon
pure vanilla extract*

2 cups milk

4 egg yolks

½ cup sugar

⅓ cup flour

*3 tablespoons unsalted
butter, cut into cubes*

1. Scrape the vanilla bean into the milk and heat with the pods and seeds in a saucepan over medium-high heat to a boil. Remove from the heat, cover, and let infuse for 10 to 15 minutes.

2. Combine the egg yolks and sugar in a bowl and beat with a whisk until light and fluffy. Add the flour and beat until smooth and fully incorporated. Slowly add about ¼ cup of the hot milk (reheated if necessary) and whisk until fully incorporated. Whisk in the remaining milk. Pour the mixture through a strainer into a saucepan.

3. Set the saucepan over medium heat and, beating continuously with a whisk, bring the mixture to a boil. Remove from the heat and, beating vigorously with a whisk, gradually add the butter cubes. Let cool for a few minutes and cover with plastic wrap, lightly pressing the plastic against the surface to prevent a skin from forming. Chill for at least 2 hours and up to 24 hours.

NECTARINE GRATIN *with* MANGO COULIS

◦ GRATIN DE NECTARINES, COULIS DE MANGUE ◦

MAKES 4 SERVINGS

Butter, for the baking pan

1½ cups granulated sugar

4 nectarines, quartered and pitted

1 ripe mango (about 1 pound), peeled and cubed

2 teaspoons freshly squeezed lemon juice

1 cup heavy cream

1 cup Pastry Cream (page 167)

Chef Thierry Faucher does not waste a drop of the syrup left over from the recipe for this wonderful fruit gratin. He uses it to coat the Candied Almonds (recipe follows) that he offers at his wine bar as a bar snack or dessert nibble.

1. Preheat the oven to 375°F and generously butter a 10-inch gratin dish or baking dish. Combine the sugar and 1½ cups water in a saucepan and heat over moderately high heat just to a boil. Lower the heat to low, add the nectarines to the simmering syrup, and poach them just until tender, 3 to 4 minutes. Transfer the nectarines from the syrup to the prepared pan with a slotted spoon. Remove the syrup from the heat and let cool.

2. Prepare the mango coulis: Combine ¼ cup of the nectarine syrup, the mango cubes, and lemon juice in a food processor or blender and puree until smooth. Refrigerate until ready to serve.

3. Heat the heavy cream in a saucepan over medium heat just to a boil. Add the pastry cream and stir with a wooden spoon until fully incorporated. Pour this mixture over the nectarines and bake just until the cream mixture turns lightly brown, 20 to 30 minutes. Remove from the oven and let settle a few minutes. Serve warm, drizzled with the cool mango coulis.

CANDIED ALMONDS
(amandes caramelisées)

1 cup nectarine syrup or substitute syrup from canned peaches

2 cups blanched slivered almonds

Preheat the oven to 350°F. Heat the nectarine syrup in a saucepan over medium heat, add the almonds, and stir until they are fully coated. Remove the almonds with a slotted spoon, transfer them to a greased baking dish, and bake in a 350°F oven, basting the almonds several times with the reserved syrup, for 20 minutes. Remove from the oven and let the candied almonds cool. Break them apart if necessary and store in an airtight container.

MELON *and* BANANA CRUMBLE

CRUMBLE AU MELON ET BANANE

MAKES 4 SERVINGS

1 cup flour

¼ granulated sugar

¼ cup brown sugar

½ cup (1 stick) unsalted butter, cut into small cubes, plus butter for the baking dish

1 medium cantaloupe, peeled and cut into 1 to 1½-inch chunks

3 bananas, cut into ½-inch slices

1 pint vanilla ice cream

The mere suggestion of baked cantaloupe may seem odd; the combination of cantaloupe and banana, more unsettling still. Yet this wine bar's house crumble, like the best cobblers, crisps, and crumbles, is an incontestible comfort food.

1. Preheat the oven to 350°F and prepare an 8 by 8-inch baking dish. Sift together the flour, granulated sugar, and brown sugar, and combine with the butter in a food processor fitted with a metal blade and pulse until the mixture begins to form clumps.

2. Lay the cantaloupe chunks on the bottom of the prepared dish and top with the banana slices. Sprinkle the crumbly topping over the fruit and bake until the topping is golden brown, 30 to 35 minutes. Let cool on a wire rack for 10 minutes and serve warm with a scoop of vanilla ice cream.

ALMOND BUTTER CAKES *with* PINEAPPLE

◦ FINANCIERS AUX ANANAS ◦

MAKES 6 SERVINGS

5 tablespoons unsalted
   butter, plus butter for the
   pan

½ cup confectioners' sugar

3 tablespoons finely ground
   blanched almonds

5 tablespoons flour

1 small pineapple (about
   3 pounds)

2 eggs

1 pint pineapple or coconut
   sorbet, optional

½ teaspoon ground
   cardamom, optional

Without a famously obsessed author to make it famous—I'm thinking of Proust and his madeleines—the buttery French tea cake known as the financier *is distinguished by the faintly nutty flavor bestowed by almond flour. Though* financiers *customarily take the shape of the shallow rectangular mini-molds in which they are baked, a round muffin pan suits them fine, especially one whose cups match the diameter of the pineapple rounds called for in Michel Rostang's recipe.*

1. Preheat the oven to 350°F.

2. To clarify the butter: Melt the butter in a saucepan over very low heat. Remove from the heat, skim the foam off the surface, and spoon the butter into a small bowl, leaving behind the milky sediment in the pan.

3. Combine the sugar, finely ground almonds, and flour in a bowl. Add the eggs and mix until thoroughly blended. Add the clarified butter and mix well.

4. Peel and slice the pineapple into 6 rounds about ¾ inch in thickness. Cut the core out of each with a knife or a small cookie cutter. Place each slice in the bottom of a buttered jumbo muffin pan (if the rounds are too wide for the pan you will have to trim them to fit). Top each with ¼ cup batter, smooth the surfaces, and bake in the oven until golden brown, 20 to 25 minutes. Cover the muffin pan with a baking sheet and, holding them together, reverse to unmold.

5. To serve, finely chop the remaining pineapple and spoon it onto six dessert plates. Top each with a pineapple *financier* and serve, if desired, with a scoop of pineapple or coconut sorbet dusted with ground cardamom.

GRAPEFRUIT *and* BANANA TART *with* SZECHUAN PEPPER ICE CREAM

◦ SABLÉ DE POMELO ET CRÈME DE BANANE, GLACE AU POIVRE DE SECHOUAN ◦

MAKES 6 SERVINGS

Unsalted butter, for the tart shell

Flour, for the tart shell

Pâte Sablée (recipe follows)

3 small pink grapefruit

¾ cup granulated sugar

2 medium (about 12 ounces) ripe bananas, sliced

2 cups vanilla ice cream

¼ to ½ teaspoon Szechuan peppercorns, toasted and crushed

A bistro chef who champions bold flavor contrasts throughout his menu, François Pasteau here attaches the intense sweetness of a creamy banana jam and a crumbly pâte sablée *(sweet short pastry) to the tartness of pink grapefruit and the pungency of Szechuan pepper ice cream. You need not make the pepper ice cream from scratch, as Pasteau does. It's far simpler to mix the pepper into—or sprinkle it atop—vanilla ice cream, as instructed here. Pasteau uses a pastry ring as a mold to shape the dough into 4-inch rounds set over a parchment paper–lined baking sheet. But the result is virtually identical using a single tart pan, as suggested here, or a half-dozen tartlet shells. Regardless of which form you choose, do not attempt to flatten the* pâte sablée *with a rolling pin: Its high butter-to-flour ratio makes the dough too fragile for that utensil, as well as for an electric mixer. The pastry should be mixed and shaped by hand. The* pâte sablée *has a crumbly, cookie-like texture that's perfect for soft toppings but preferably not juicy fruit ones. The dough may be flavored with vanilla, lemon zest, rum, or cinnamon.*

The banana jam makes for a terrific dessert crêpe filling or dessert topping for yogurt, ice cream, or pound cake.

1. Preheat the oven to 350°F. Butter and flour a 9 to 10-inch tart pan or straight-sided cake pan and tap out the excess flour. Place the *pâte sablée* dough in the tart pan and flatten it out with your fingers to form a flat, even layer about ½ inch thick (do not spread the dough up the sides of the pan). Bake until very lightly browned around the edges and pale golden on top, 11 to 12 minutes. Transfer to a cooling rack.

2. Peel the grapefruit, separate them into sections, and drain them on paper towels to remove any excess juices.

3. Place the sugar and 2 tablespoons water in a saucepan over moderately high heat, stirring occasionally and scraping down the sides with a wooden spoon. When the mixture begins to turn caramel in color, add the banana slices, heat to a boil, and beat vigorously with a whisk until all the banana slices have dissolved. Set aside and let cool.

4. A half hour or less before serving, spread an even layer of the banana jam over the pastry crust. Arrange the grapefruit sections atop the banana in a circular pattern. Cut into triangular slices and serve with a scoop of vanilla ice cream mixed or sprinkled lightly, if desired, with crushed Szechuan pepper.

PÂTE SABLÉE
(sweet short pastry)

YIELDS ENOUGH DOUGH FOR
A 10-INCH TART

2 tablespoons blanched
  almonds

1/2 teaspoon granulated
  sugar

10 tablespoons unsalted
  butter, softened

1/2 cup confectioners' sugar

2 egg yolks

1 cup flour

1. Place the almonds and granulated sugar in a food processor fitted with the metal blade and grind just until they turn into a granular powder.

2. Combine the butter, confectioners' sugar, and egg yolks in a bowl and mix with your fingertips just until the mixture is homogeneous. Gradually add the almond powder and then the flour, mixing with your fingertips until fully incorporated. Do not overwork the dough. Roll the dough into a smooth, compact ball, flatten it slightly, wrap well in plastic wrap, and refrigerate for at least 2 hours and up to 1 week, or store in the freezer up to 1 month.

3. Thaw in the refrigerator and don't remove until ready to use.

WARM CHOCOLATE BLINIS

◦ BLINIS AU CHOCOLAT ◦

MAKES 4 TO 5 SERVINGS
(ABOUT 16 BLINIS)

7 ounces bittersweet
chocolate, finely chopped

6 tablespoons unsalted
butter, plus 1 tablespoon
melted butter for the skillet

3 egg yolks

6 egg whites

1/4 cup sugar

1 pint vanilla ice cream or
crème fraîche

1 cup Raspberry Sauce
(recipe follows)

These delectable little chocolate pancakes provide the fanfare expected of great brasserie desserts. They possess the shape and ceremony of Russian blini, the expectation of a molten flourless chocolate cake, and the spine-tingling opposites—gooey/creamy, hot/cold—of a warm brownie ice cream sundae.

1. Heat the chocolate in the top of a double boiler, stirring once or twice with a wooden spoon, until fully melted. Add the butter and gently stir until melted and fully incorporated. Remove from the heat, let cool for 10 minutes, and then stir in the egg yolks, one at a time, until fully incorporated.

2. Place the egg whites in a mixing bowl and beat vigorously with an electric mixer or whisk until the whites are frothy. Add the sugar and beat until stiff peaks form. Fold the eggs whites into the chocolate mixture and gently stir just until fully blended.

3. Heat a large nonstick skillet over medium heat. Lower the heat just slightly and brush the skillet with 1 tablespoon melted butter. Pour 1 tablespoon of the chocolate batter into the skillet for each blini, spacing them at least an inch apart, and cook until the surface bubbles and the underside begins to brown, 3 to 4 minutes. Carefully turn the blinis using a thin spatula, and cook until browned on the other side, about 1 minute. Transfer to a plate and keep them warm in a low oven while you cook the remaining blinis, brushing the pan with a little butter when necessary. Serve 3 or 4 blinis to a plate, top with a small scoop of vanilla ice cream or crème fraîche, and drizzle the plate, if desired, with raspberry sauce.

RASPBERRY SAUCE
(coulis de framboise)

....

YIELDS 2 CUPS

3 cups fresh or frozen unsweetened raspberries

½ cup sugar

2 tablespoons freshly squeezed lemon juice

Combine the ingredients in a food processor and process until smooth. Pass through a strainer, pushing down on the pureed berries with the back of a spoon to remove the seeds. Refrigerate until ready to serve, up to 2 days.

MOLTEN CHOCOLATE CAKE

◦ PALET MI-CUIT AU CHOCOLAT ◦

MAKES 6 SERVINGS

6 tablespoons butter, plus
   butter for the muffin tin

Confectioners' sugar, for the
   muffin tin

6 ounces bittersweet
   chocolate, finely chopped

3 egg yolks

3 whole eggs

¾ cup granulated sugar

½ cup flour

Raspberry Sauce
   (page 175)

Mi-cuit *("half-baked"), a cooking term applied to foie gras and, less frequently, tuna and salmon, is an apt description of this exceptionally runny rendition of a* moelleux au chocolat—*warm chocolate cake. Once pierced with a fork, Clémentine's* palet *("disk") slowly discharges its molten core of dark chocolate. You can bake your cakes in 4 to 5-inch pastry rings, as they do at Clémentine, or in a jumbo muffin pan, as suggested here.*

1. Generously butter 6 cups of a jumbo muffin pan (or 6 ramekins or custard cups) and then dust the cups with confectioners' sugar, tapping out any excess sugar.

2. Heat the chocolate in the top of a double boiler, stirring once or twice with a wooden spoon, until fully melted. Add the butter and gently stir until melted and fully incorporated. Remove from the heat.

3. Combine the egg yolks and whole eggs in a saucepan and beat gently with a whisk until blended. Add the granulated sugar and heat over low heat, stirring gently (do not whip the mixture), just until warm, 2 to 3 minutes.

4. Sift the flour into the melted chocolate until completely incorporated. Fold the egg mixture into the chocolate mixture and stir, making sure to scrape up all the chocolate from the bottom of the pan, until fully blended. Divide the batter equally among the muffin cups (they should be about one-third full), cover with plastic wrap, and refrigerate for at least 1 hour or until ready to bake (the batter will keep for several days).

5. Preheat the oven to 425°F. Place the muffin pan (or a baking sheet topped with ramekins) in the oven and bake until the edges

are puffed and the center jiggles only slightly when the pan is gently shaken, 11 to 12 minutes or, if the batter has been chilled for several hours, up to 13 minutes. Remove from the oven and immediately unmold the cakes: Work a small sharp knife around the perimeter between the cakes and molds. Place a baking sheet over the muffin pan and, holding the sheet and pan together, reverse to unmold the cakes. Use a thin spatula to transfer the cakes to 6 individual dessert plates. Serve immediately with Raspberry Sauce or Orange Caramel Sauce (page 163), ice cream, whipped cream, a fruit sorbet, or custard sauce.

PARIS-BREST

MAKES 6 SERVINGS

1 cup (2 sticks) unsalted
butter, at room
temperature

1¼ cups ground Praline
(recipe follows)

2 cups Pastry Cream
(page 167), chilled

1 recipe Choux Pastry
(page 21)

¼ cup chopped blanched
almonds

¼ cup confectioners' sugar

According to legend, this pastry classic was created around the turn of the twentieth century by a patisserie situated along the route of the classic bicycle race that connects the cities of Paris and Brest. The true name of the race and route is Paris-Brest-Paris. Its dessert homage is assembled by splitting a choux pastry horizontally and filling it with praline buttercream. The pastry, like the race, carries special significance for Thierry Breton, a native of Brest (which is in the region of Brittany in northwest France) and a cycling fanatic. When dinner service at his bistro is complete and the very last Paris-Brest has been consumed, Breton hops on a racing bike and speeds out of the 10th arrondissement on midnight training rides. Although the Paris-Brest is typically ring-shaped to suggest a wheel, Breton simplifies its preparation and presentation by shaping individual rounds of choux pastry which, once baked and puffed, have a slightly irregular shape not unlike that of the city where the Paris-Brest-Paris begins and ends.

1. To prepare the praline cream filling: Beat the butter with an electric mixer until smooth. Add the praline and beat until fully incorporated. Add the pastry cream and beat until thick and fluffy, about 5 minutes. Cover and refrigerate for at least 3 hours and up to 24 hours.

2. Preheat the oven to 400°F. Line a baking sheet with parchment paper. Prepare the choux pastry. Form 3-inch balls of pastry in one of two ways: Either fill a pastry bag with the dough and pipe out balls onto the lined baking sheet spaced at least 2 inches apart or accomplish the same by using one soup spoon to gather the pastry and another to push it onto the sheet. Bake for 20 minutes, shut off the oven, and let them sit for an additional 10 minutes. Remove from the oven and let cool.

3. Carefully cut off the top halves of the puffs using small scissors or a knife. Spoon the praline cream mixture into a pastry bag with a fluted ¾-inch tip and pipe onto the bottom halves of the puffs in a tight spiral, starting at the middle and working outward to the rim. Scatter the chopped almonds over the cream, replace the tops, sprinkle the top with confectioners' sugar, and serve.

PRALINE

YIELDS 1½ CUPS

Vegetable oil
⅔ cup sugar
¼ cup toasted almonds
¼ cup toasted hazelnuts

Lightly oil a rimmed baking sheet. Combine the sugar and 3 tablespoons water in a saucepan over low heat and stir with a wooden spoon until the sugar dissolves. Add the almonds and hazelnuts, increase the heat to medium-high, and cook, stirring occasionally, until the mixture turns a deep caramel color, about 6 minutes. Pour the mixture onto the prepared baking sheet and let cool completely. Break the praline clusters into pieces and grind to a powder in a food processor or blender. Store in an airtight container.

CHOCOLATE PROFITEROLES

◦ PROFITEROLES AU CHOCOLAT ◦

1 recipe Choux Pastry
   (page 21)

1 egg

8 ounces semisweet or
   bittersweet chocolate,
   broken into small pieces

¾ cup light cream

1 pint vanilla ice cream

The instant profiteroles are served, all conversation stops. The waiter's pouring of the warm chocolate sauce from a silver pot over the ice cream-filled pastry puffs is a brasserie ritual to be observed without distraction. The expectant diner must subsequently break into the profiteroles immediately, when the contrast between hot and cold is greatest. Only later should he or she feel at liberty to remark on the appearance of the classic dessert, which bears the same black-and-white color scheme as the uniformed waiter who serves it (see page 142).

1. Preheat the oven to 400°F. Line a baking sheet with parchment paper.

2. Form 1½ to 2-inch balls of the choux pastry in one of two ways: Either fill a pastry bag with the dough and pipe out balls onto the lined baking sheet spaced at least an inch apart, or accomplish the same by using one soup spoon to gather the pastry and another to push it onto the sheet. Beat the egg with 1 teaspoon cold water and brush this egg wash over the top halves of each ball. Bake for 20 minutes, shut off the oven, and let heat for an additional 10 minutes. Remove from the oven and set aside on sheets to cool, at least 20 minutes.

3. Before serving, place the chocolate in the top of a double boiler set over medium-high heat and cook until the chocolate is melted. Heat the cream in a saucepan over medium heat, pour it into the chocolate, and stir with a wooden spoon until smooth and uniform in color and heated through. Cover to keep warm.

4. Carefully cut off the top halves of the puffs using small scissors or a knife, fill the bottoms with a small scoop of vanilla ice cream, and replace the tops.

5. To serve, place 3 puffs on each plate and douse at the table with warm chocolate sauce.

KOUGLOF

MAKES 6 SERVINGS
(1 CAKE)

1 cup raisins

½ cup rum

6 tablespoons milk

¼ cup granulated sugar

1 envelope dry yeast

8 tablespoons unsalted
butter, at room
temperature, plus butter
for the pan

2 eggs

2½ cups flour, plus flour for
the work surface

1 teaspoon salt

½ cup blanched slivered
almonds

Confectioners' sugar

The variety of spellings—kugelhupf, kougelhof, gougelhof, gugelhuph, etc.—applied to this sweetened yeast bread reflects its popularity throughout central Europe. But it is its Alsatian heritage that makes the region's almond and raisin-filled counterpart to French brioche and Italian panettone a natural fit for Parisian brasseries such as La Coupole, where it is served both in a breakfast bread basket and as the foundation for French toast (page 183), and Bofinger, where it is occasionally featured with fruit preserves as a dessert special. This recipe for the ring-shaped k-o-u-g-l-o-f is my adaptation of the kouglof baked for Bofinger and La Coupole.

1. Hours before: Sprinkle the raisins with rum and let macerate for at least 2 hours.

2. Heat the milk in a saucepan but do not allow it to boil. Remove from the heat, add 1 tablespoon granulated sugar, mix well, and let cool. Sprinkle the yeast over the mixture, stir briefly with a fork or a whisk, and let stand until the liquid foams, about 10 minutes.

3. Meanwhile, place the butter in the bowl of an electric mixer and beat until smooth. Gradually add the remaining granulated sugar and beat until light and fluffy. Add the eggs, one at a time, beating well. Add the milk-yeast mixture and blend well. Gradually mix in the flour and salt and beat until you have a homogeneous mixture. Drain the raisins, add to the dough, and mix until evenly distributed.

4. Remove the dough from the mixer, gather into a mass, and knead on a floured work surface, working the dough in a circular motion with your palms, for 5 minutes.

5. Generously butter a 12-cup fluted ring mold or a Bundt pan and scatter the almonds on the bottom of the pan. Lightly dust the center of the dough ball with flour. Using your fingertips, make a small

hole in the center and gently stretch from all sides, enlarging the hole just enough to fit over the tube in the center of the Bundt pan. Lay the ring of dough in the pan over the almonds, cover with a towel, and set aside at room temperature until the dough has risen to the top of the pan, about 1 hour.

6. Preheat the oven to 375°F. Bake the kouglof until golden brown, about 45 minutes. Immediately unmold it onto a rack and let cool. Sprinkle with confectioners' sugar and serve.

KOUGLOF FRENCH TOAST

◦ PAIN PERDU DE KOUGLOF ◦

MAKES 6 DESSERT
SERVINGS OR 4 BRUNCH
SERVINGS

1 recipe Kouglof (page 181)
or substitute brioche,
panettone, or challah

3 eggs

¼ cup granulated sugar

1 cup milk

1 cup light cream

2 teaspoons pure vanilla
extract

3 tablespoons unsalted
butter or more as needed

Use slightly stale and thus extra absorbant kouglof to soak up the eggs, milk, and cream in the recipe of Paul Delbard, the brasserie's pastry chef, and the divinely moist and fluffy result is something closer to an afternoon bread pudding or an evening soufflé than a morning French toast.

1. Cut the kouglof into triangular wedges about 2 inches in width at their widest part.

2. Combine the eggs and sugar in a shallow pan and beat with a whisk until well blended. Add the milk, cream, and vanilla and whisk until fully blended.

3. Dunk as many wedges of kouglof that will fit into the pan in a single layer and let them soak, turning once, for 3 to 5 minutes. Lift the soaked wedges with a slotted spatula to let the excess liquid drain off back into the pan and transfer to a large plate. Repeat until the remaining wedges have been soaked.

4. Melt the butter in a large skillet over medium heat. Add the kouglof wedges and cook until golden brown, 2 to 3 minutes on each side. If preparing in batches, place the finished wedges on a sheet pan and keep them warm in a 250°F oven. Add more butter to the skillet as needed.

5. Serve hot with fruit jam, berries, maple syrup, crème anglaise, or vanilla ice cream.

CRÊPES ALEXANDRE

MAKES 4 SERVINGS

2 oranges

1 lemon

⅓ cup Grand Marnier or orange liqueur

Twelve 8-inch Dessert Crêpes (recipe follows)

6 tablespoons sugar

4 tablespoons (½ stick) unsalted butter

Gallopin may have opened in 1876, but its crêpes Alexandre, a stirring interpretation of classic crêpes Suzette, did not arrive until Georges Alexandre, the former owner of Bofinger, bought the brasserie in 1997. Although the flambéing is central to the performance, it is not crucial to the finished dish. If you'd rather not flambé, after you've added the Grand Marnier and let its alcohol bubble off, sprinkle the crêpes with sugar and set under the broiler to caramelize.

1. The day before you plan to serve, grate the zest of the oranges and lemon. Cut the grated oranges in half, squeeze their juice, and store in the refrigerator. Soak the orange zest and lemon zest in the Grand Marnier overnight.

2. Drain the zest from the Grand Marnier and reserve both.

3. Prepare the crêpes.

4. Heat 3 tablespoons sugar in a very wide saucepan over high heat. When the sugar begins to melt, add the butter, orange zest, and lemon zest. Spear a lemon section with a fork and use it to stir the mixture (the lemon detaches the sugar from the pan and flavors it). When the mixture begins to caramelize and turn golden, add the orange juice, heat to a boil, and beat with a whisk until reduced to a syrup, 3 to 5 minutes.

5. Fold each crêpe in quarters and carefully place them in the pan, fanning the folded crêpes around the pan and basting them with the syrup. Sprinkle the crêpes with the remaining sugar, pour the Grand Marnier over the crêpes, let cook for a couple of seconds until the liqueur bubbles, and carefully set aflame with a long match (or see headnote if you'd rather not flambé). When the flames have died down, serve the crêpes 3 to a plate, generously spooning the sauce over them.

DESSERT CRÊPES
(crêpes sucrées)

....

MAKES A DOZEN 8-INCH
CRÊPES

1 cup flour

1 cup milk

2 eggs, beaten

¼ teaspoon salt

2 tablespoons melted butter,
plus melted butter for the
pan

1½ tablespoons sugar

1 tablespoon orange liqueur
or rum

1. Pour the flour into a mixing bowl, make a well in the center, pour half the milk into the well, and stir with a wooden spatula or spoon until fully incorporated.

2. Whisk the eggs, salt, butter, and sugar into the flour mixture. Gradually pour in the remaining milk and mix until perfectly smooth, adding a tiny bit more milk if necessary to thin the batter. Stir in the liqueur, cover, and set aside at room temperature for 30 minutes to 1 hour.

3. Heat an 8-inch crêpe pan over moderately heat. Brush the bottom of the pan with melted butter. Pour about ¼ cup batter into the middle of the pan and swirl the pan in all directions to coat the entire pan with a thin layer, pouring the excess batter back into the bowl. Cook the crêpe until brown around the edges and light brown on the bottom, 45 seconds to 1 minute. Using a thin spatula loosen the edges of the crêpe, then flip it and cook on the other side for 15 to 20 seconds. Let cool slightly on a rack before stacking the crêpes on a plate. If using the crêpes on a later date, wrap the stacked crêpes in plastic wrap and refrigerate for up to 2 days or freeze for up to 1 month.

The Paris of Parisians

✳

THE ESSENTIALS

BISTROS

L'AMI JEAN

27, rue Malar; 7th
01 47 05 86 89
Métro: La Tour Maubourg
(pages 120, 129, 132)

There's no longer a Basque at this seventy-year-old, tavern-styled, deceptively humble Basque bistro situated midway between the Champs de Mars and the Invalides. There's not even a guy named Jean. Yet new chef-owner Stéphane Jégo, a native of Brittany, devotes an entire menu section to specialties of the French Basque country. *Plats du jour*, however, forgo regional loyalties and are determined instead by two considerations: what seasonal foods sold at the Rungis wholesale markets catch Jégo's eye or that of the other chefs in the same clique, and what he is inspired to do with those ingredients. It's the high-minded, low-priced, market-driven, French southwest–leaning bistro cuisine he mastered in the employ of Yves Camdeborde at the acclaimed La Régalade. Jégo takes rustic, humble, down-market foods (off-cuts

of meat, oily fish, root vegetables, pulses) into his kitchen and finds their inner beauty. What exits via the pass-through could be mistaken for highly accomplished haute cuisine were it served on fine china.

L'AVANT-GOÛT

26, rue Bobillot; 13th
01 53 80 24 00
Métro: Place d'Italie
(pages 78, 145, 146, 147)

"I adore art," says Christophe Beaufront, a bistro chef some have accused of being an artist. "The difference is that food should not be difficult to understand. It must stay simple and true to the culture of *terroir* [meaning its native soil, its origins]." Even so, his cooking at L'Avant-Goût, French for "foretaste," is hardly indifferent to the avant-garde. He freely fits contemporary whims into classic bistro cooking, fusing new flavor combinations and letting sweets and savories trespass the customary borders between them. Vanilla infuses main courses; parsley, a dessert sorbet. Beaufront is both beneficiary and victim of his signature main course, a *pot au feu* recast with pork offal in place of beef, sweet potatoes substituting for plain spuds, and fennel bulbs standing in for turnips. The dish turns up in blurbs and reviews as reliably as the bistro's phone number, stealing attention from newer creations like his bittersweet Endive Curry Soup with Carrots and Mussels (page 78). L'Avant-Goût lacks the smoky, noisy, dirty conditions that supposedly give cramped, good-valued bistros their character. Beaufront nevertheless applauds informality, boasting of the diner who so enjoyed his *pot au feu* that he lifted the near-empty casserole to his mouth and drank broth from it.

LE BEURRE NOISETTE

68, rue Vasco-de-Gama; 15th
01 48 56 82 49
Métro: Lourmel, Porte de Versailles
(pages 109, 111, 131, 158)

❀ ❀ ❀ ❀ ❀ ❀ ❀ ❀ ❀ ❀ ❀ ❀ ❀ ❀ ❀ ❀ ❀ ❀

Spend but five minutes with Thierry Blanqui and it becomes apparent why he was never going to make it as an executive chef at a grand Parisian restaurant like Ledoyen, his last employer. He's too gentle. To effectively lead a Michelin multistarred kitchen brigade a chef must be talented, demanding, and, when necessary, tyrannical. It isn't only egg whites that must be whipped into shape. Aware that he lacked the requisite mean gene, Blanqui broke from three-star chef Christian Le Squer, his long-standing and presumably bossier colleague, and retreated to the southeast tip of the Left Bank to open this quiet, lovely, gently priced bistro. Le Beurre Noisette's cooking, with its slow-cooked meats, robust ragouts, and bold flavors, is not timid in any way. But the soft side of Blanqui's personality is manifest in the patient care he gives to the preparation and assembly of each *plat du jour*, now that there is no one around to yell at or to be yelled at by, save for the odd, ill-tempered diner.

LE BISTROT DES CAPUCINS

27, avenue Gambetta; 20th
01 46 36 74 75
Métro: Gambetta, Père Lachaise
(pages 70, 94, 139, 162)

❀ ❀ ❀ ❀ ❀ ❀ ❀ ❀ ❀ ❀ ❀ ❀ ❀ ❀ ❀ ❀ ❀ ❀

Finding a chef as accomplished as Gérard Fouché in a bistro as modest and remote and as close to the graveyard as this—Le Bistrot des Capucins faces the Père Lachaise cemetery—demands an explanation. After cooking for such greats as André Guillot, Roger Vergé, Michel Rostang, and Jacques Cagna and rising to the position of chef de cuisine at Le Grand Véfour, Fouché decided he was seeing too much of his corporate bosses and not enough of his daughter. He decided to go it alone, first in the Paris suburb of Saint-Mandé and finally here. The rugby paraphernalia hung on the walls does little to reassure first-time diners, and neither does the notoriously impish waiter who is Fouché's sidekick. No diner—at least no diner who understands French—is spared the barbs of a *serveur* inflicted with a Figaro complex, an insatiable and distinctly Parisian (though the character is Italian, his creator, Pierre-Augustin Caron de Beaumarchais, was Parisian) desire to mock those he serves. The other peculiarity of this bistro is that Fouché hates waiting of any kind. You get the impression that the espressos are served very hot just so the sugar cubes will dissolve more quickly. Gaps between courses are brief. Most embrace these conditions with little delay. Southwest French cuisine has moved to the forefront of the Parisian dining scene, and few bistro chefs do it better than Fouché.

LE BISTROT D'À CÔTÉ

16, rue Gustave Flaubert; 17th
01 42 67 05 81
Métro; Ternes
(pages 50, 171)

It was an old rule of real estate, as much as a new vision of dining, that led Michel Rostang to become the first star chef in Paris to open a bistro annex, as lower-rent spin-offs of high-end restaurants are categorized, in 1987. "I was always told," explains Rostang, "that when the space next to you opens up you buy it first and figure out what to do with it after." So when the Belle Époque dairy shop next to his elegant, eponymous restaurant became vacant he bought it, restored its vintage woodwork, marble fixtures, and reverse-painted glass, filled its shelves with his fine collection of French *barbotine* (glazed pottery), and opened Le Bistrot d'à Côté—"the Bistro Next Door." Its attraction, then as now, was the chance to eat Rostang's imposing food at a third or less of the price in an informal setting. An important distinction that separates this annex from others that followed it, including three more Rostang bistros, is that it features French country cooking as opposed to formulaic and soulless knockoffs of a famous chef's cutting-edge cuisine. Moreover, its close proximity to the parent restaurant suggests that the food is effectively coming from the same kitchen, even if the attention of Rostang himself is focused on newer ventures.

LE BISTROT PAUL BERT

18, rue Paul Bert; 11th
01 43 72 24 01
Métro: Faidherbe Chaligny
(pages 100, 138)

The Paul Bert takes its name from its street, its personality from its gregarious owner, and its ideas from that gregarious owner's favorite bistros and wine bars. Opened in 1996 on a not-yet-gentrified block in the 11th arrondissement, it is a rarity among retro bistros done up in a hodgepodge of old signage, vintage fixtures, and timeworn furnishings in that it appeals to hard-core old-timers and bourgeois bohemians alike, even as the latter crowd out the former. These disparate groups regard Bertrand Auboyneau, the former stockbroker who produced this smoke-and-mirrors act, as one of their own. It is a testament to this large man's social dexterity and maybe also the fact that few have seen who he hangs out with in his spare time and where they go (it isn't to Yoga class, that's for sure). He and his fellow bistro bums, most employed in the trade, travel a circuit of preferred addresses, several of which are represented in the book. The wines, dishes, and fine seasonal ingredients discovered during these jaunts inform the solid but unfussy menu at the Paul Bert, so much so that Auboyneau could be accused of property theft were these ideas not lifted with the permission and even the encouragement of their originators. What did I tell you about this guy's social dexterity? Chef Thierry Laurent's *steak frites*, though possibly the best in Paris, remains an unlisted dish. Because Laurent can turn out only so many *frites* from the old cast-iron pan he uses to fry small batches of them, they are featured irregularly and only as an accompaniment for steak tartare. Demands for pan-fried (not raw) steak and *frites* are entertained by request only.

LE CHANTEFABLE

93, avenue Gambetta; 20th
01 46 36 81 76
Métro: Gambetta
(page 166)

With twenty-seven wines to sample by the glass at an exquisite marble counter, Le Chantefable could fairly call itself a wine bar. Continuous service, shucked-to-order oysters, curve-topped mirrors, ornate moldings, and stork-necked brass beer taps would justify its carrying the label of a brasserie. Then again, casual terrace tables that accommodate both short-term (e.g., 5 minutes) and long-term (e.g., 5 hours) occupancy would ordinarily earmark the establishment as a café. Yet proprietor Pierre Ayral asserts that Le Chantefable is a bistro, partly because it is that, too, but mostly because he thinks that's what will attract students, bourgeois bohemians, and other new settlers of the 20th arrondissement. As the owner of an unapologetically unstylish brasserie on the Paris periphery that's wildly popular with seniors, Ayral worries the term *brasserie* will turn off his younger, hipper clientele. "We take the brasserie system and apply a bistro spirit," explained Ayral when, to his displeasure, I uttered the wrong "B" word inside Le Chantefable. "Look at the service. Look at the setting. It's a bistro." He has a point. The servers are casual in dress and manner. The robust *plats du jour* scribbled on the slate board bespeak a bistro. Ultimately, Le Chantefable is whatever you want it to be. Behind wrought-iron French doors, the restored and refitted Art Nouveau interior is spectacular for its lack of spectacle. The surfaces are unpolished; the lighting, dim. The food, given the casual setting and versatile program, is always better than you expect it to be. Chef Laurent Aulard can wow you with a seasonal classic from the annals of French gastronomy or a composed salad. Ayral is a well-connected native of Aveyron, the home region of Roquefort cheese and many a Parisian restaurateur, and he knows his meat and potatoes. You won't get a bad steak or bad *frite* at Le Chantefable, even if you call it a brasserie.

CHEZ GEORGES

1, rue du Mail; 2nd
01 42 60 07 11
Métro: Sentier
(page 104)

The habitués at Chez Georges probably don't like it much when host-owner Bernard Brouillet gets a haircut. They depend upon his bistro for its aversion to even the slightest change, and might lose their equilibrium were Brouillet's barber to take a few millimeters too much off the back. The menu posted on the wall is from 1960, the year of Chez

Georges's opening, but only its prices, wine vintages, and faded ink distinguish it much from the current edition. In truth, today's classics-only menu, with its grilled turbot in thick béarnaise sauce, baked fillet of sole in unctuous cream sauce, veal chop in morel mushroom cream sauce, and pan-grilled sirloin in a Cognac mustard cream sauce (are you seeing a theme yet?), is comparable to the one penned by Georges Constant, Bernard's father-in-law, for Au Roi Gourmet, the nearby restaurant his family operated at the place des Victoires for three generations prior to conceiving Chez Georges. The time warp is reinforced by swift yet accommodating servers who, though not yet middle-aged, resemble characters from a 1930s Marcel Carné classic of French cinema. Older looking still is the odd but nevertheless indispensible painting of a *jeu de mail* (the French forerunner of golf was once played where the rue du Mail now sits) that covers ten seat lengths of the front dining-room wall. It was acquired by Georges and Bernard from the space's prior tenant for the sum of zero francs. They feigned disinterest and refused the owner's offer to sell, betting correctly it would be too difficult, both physically and emotionally, to remove the framed mural from the premises.

CHEZ MICHEL

10, rue de Belzunce; 10th
01 44 53 06 20
Métro: Gare du Nord, Poissonnière
(pages 76, 95, 178)

Chez Michel is so good a bistro it has even made the rue de Belzunce, a short, gray, and otherwise obscure street behind the church of Saint Vincent de Paul, famous. In truth the street enjoyed some notoriety for its resident restaurant (in 1980 it garnered two Michelin stars) from 1939 until 1995, the year its kitchen was taken over for the first time by an acclaimed chef not named Michel. Thierry Breton, an upstart from Brittany who had rapidly climbed the kitchen ranks at the Hotel Ritz, the Hôtel Royale Monceau, the Relais au Louis XIII, the Tour d'Argent, the Hôtel de Crillon, and Lapérouse, purchased Chez Michel and downgraded its menu and mission to bistro class. "The idea was to do serious cuisine without taking ourselves too seriously," recalls Breton, then twenty-six. The informality lets the extroverted protégé of master chefs Guy Legay, Manual Martinez, and Christian Constant roam the main floor and cellar dining areas and schmooze, a freedom he had not enjoyed before. "I am not capable of being confined to the kitchen," he says. "I need contact; I want to see the dining room." His menu reads like a gourmet bike tour through the coast and countryside of Brittany, highlighting the region's most prized food products by indicating their place of origin—the *Saint Pierre* (John Dory fish) of Guilvinec, the *coucou* (chicken) of Rennes (page 95), the *cidre* (cider) of Cornouaille—and then showing them off to best advantage through precision cooking and exquisite garnishes, which, like *sel* (salt) of Guérande, enhance but don't hide the natural flavors. His signature dessert, a Paris-Brest, is a classic pastry named for the bicycle race that, like Chez Michel, connects the French capital to the heart of Brittany.

CLÉMENTINE

5, rue Saint-Marc; 2nd
01 40 41 05 65
Métro: Bourse, Richelieu Drouot
(pages 63, 176)

Too homey and homely to be a re-creation, this authentic bistro is nonetheless a product of two vintages separated by ninety years. The black glass panel on the storefront of number 5 rue Saint-Marc, like the words reverse-painted on it in the style of the Belle Époque, *"VINS RESTAURANTS À LA CARTE," "PLAT DU JOUR," "SPÉCIALITÉ DE VINS DE TOURAINE,"* dates from 1903. The name Clémentine and the house ban on rice, pasta, *frites*, and politics were adopted in 1993 when Franck Langrenne, formerly a cook at the three-Michelin-starred Lucas Carton, became the bistro's fifth owner. You're unlikely to find the deliciously humble Clémentine on any top ten dining list for the 2nd arrondissement, much less for *tout* Paris, and yet when the affable Langrenne is looking after you, delivering solid if unspectacular food paired with amusing if unremarkable barbs, there

is no possibility of regret. Langrenne and chef Franck Charton enforce what amounts to a fifth ban: no white space on their lunch and dinner plates. Every *plat du jour* is crowded with four side courses, including a memorable Jerusalem artichoke puree if you and that root vegetable happen to be in season. The two Francks' *palet mi-cuit au chocolat*, an exceptionally oozy warm chocolate cake, is timed to the second. It never misses.

LE DAUPHIN

167, rue Saint-Honoré; 1st
01 42 60 40 11
Métro: Palais Royale Musée du Louvre
(pages 33, 53, 124, 165)

"We're not a *bistro* bistro," concedes Le Dauphin co-chef/owner Didier Oudill. "You open a Beaujolais, put out some shredded carrots, some herring, that's a true bistro." Be that as it may, Oudill and partner Edgar Duhr's duplex near the Louvre, the Comédie-Française, and the Palais-Royale has fostered several new and influential expressions of rustic bistro cooking. They were among the first in Paris to devote an entire menu section to *parrilladas* (mixed grills prepared *à la plancha*, over a super-hot, ungreased griddle), to assemble and serve cold shared appetizers in sterilized jars, and to present braised meats on the table in small, cast-iron Staub cocottes, now a widespread bistro fashion. "It is better to be copied than to copy," remarks Oudill, his bittersweet tone indicating that he is as much angered as he is flattered by his imitators. Befitting its cuisine and outlook, Le Dauphin doesn't look like a bistro but it does have a bistro look thanks to handsome globe lights, frosted-glass partitions, and Art Deco ornamentation in wood and iron. Oak tables covered with tan runners have built-in holes for conical olive oil and vinegar bottles. Though pricey even for a bistro that isn't a *bistro* bistro, Le Dauphin's set menus offer excellent value and, contrary to the norm, little compromise.

L'ENTREDGEU

83, rue de Laugier; 17th
01 30 54 97 24
Métro: Porte de Champerret
(pages 23, 41)

No longer is it *scandaleux* when a promising chef quits a hard-won post in the state-of-the-art kitchen at a Michelin-multistarred restaurant to operate a low-budget bistro. But it is rare for an accomplished member of the dining-room staff to take a comparable plunge. If you've worked in the front of the house for three-star chefs like Joël Robuchon, Alain Ducasse, and Alain Passard, as Pénélope Tredgeu has, then giving up the staff meals would already seem to constitute too great a sacrifice. Madame Tredgeu was nevertheless tired of *haute gastronomie* and the relentless perfectionism it demands. She and her similarly accomplished but restless husband, chef Philippe Tredgeu, found a neglected two-room café space roughly the size of a one-bedroom apartment, on the outer edge of northwest Paris, restored its back bar's marble counter and mahogany compartments, mounted some cut-cornered octagonal mirrors and contemporary still life canvases on the walls, and refashioned the concept of a mom-and-pop bistro. L'Entredgeu's homey simplicity and elbow-to-elbow conviviality fit right in. Its food, however, is a good deal more elaborate and sophisticated than the surroundings would suggest—"not

too bistro, not too gastro," according to Monsieur Tredgeu, who like other chefs of his generation insists it's the ingredients that make the cuisine. Even so, he is sufficiently skilled, creative, and worldly to keep even his most discerning diners captivated, not least of all Madame Tredgeu herself. If staff meals at L'Entredgeu are composed of pop's extras or leftovers they cannot possibly be disagreeable.

L'ÉPI DUPIN

11, rue Dupin; 6th
01 42 22 64 56
Métro: Sèvres—Babylone
(pages 36, 58, 118, 172)

Chef-owner François Pasteau's basic formula for L'Épi Dupin, first put into practice in 1995, is comparable to that of just about every good-valued gastro bistro to open in Paris since: Bring in high-quality cuisine while preserving the low prices and congenial, convivial, and congested conditions of a true bistro. But Pasteau added originality as a prerequisite, insisting his menu feature things not available elsewhere. And so, although his desire to ennoble low-end foods like mackerel and chicken wings is no longer unique, his means of doing so usually are. In particular, Pasteau's amusing habit of mixing very sweet flavors with savory and acidic ones takes L'Épi Dupin out of the culinary conversation transpiring among more traditionally minded bistro chefs. His honeyed endive *tatin* with goat cheese (page 36), for example, positions him and his fortunate diners outside the mainstream. His sesame-crusted fried mussels are cushioned by a sweet potato puree, hardly a typically French combination. These and other signature dishes are expertly described and appraised by a team of otherwise rushed waiters who are a big part of the L'Épi Dupin experience. Habitués know to keep on the best of terms with Loïc, the boyish team leader who appears to run this perennially sold-out show.

AUX LYONNAIS

32, rue Saint-Marc; 2nd
01 42 96 65 04
Métro: Richelieu Drouot
(pages 97, 135)

⁂

Several talented young chefs featured in this book claim to have benefited from the limitations built into the bistro trade and the resourcefulness forced upon them. Alain Ducasse wanted to test the opposite hypothesis: What would happen, the famed chef must have wondered, if he fitted one of his protégés into the kitchen as well as the framework of a traditional bistro and let him work with the finest ingredients, equipment, and techniques available in twenty-first-century Paris? Aux Lyonnais's answer is routinely remarkable reinterpretations of the most basic bistro cuisine. The cooking style at the handsomely restored period bistro is as much Ducassian as it is Lyonnaise, and thus preciously close to a contradiction. A great passion for tradition that rules out exotic ingredients, unorthodox flavor combinations, and fusion of any kind is expressed through modern, nontraditional means. Cooking with utter transparency is the obsession of chef David Rathgeber, a brilliant Ducasse disciple who eschews any flourish that might diminish or distort the essential flavor of his ingredients, Thickening a *jus* with flour is unthinkable. So, too, is boiling spring vegetables for a casserole when sautéing them, one *légume* at a

time, sets in a more concentrated flavor. The downside of Aux Lyonnais, though some may not see it as one, is that perfection is no substitute for personality. Casual warmth and bistro hominess are severely lacking.

NATACHA

17 bis, rue Campagne-Première; 14th
01 43 20 79 27
Métro: Raspail
(pages 20, 47, 105, 130)

⁂

A stylish bistro with a cult following, Natacha both feeds off and sustains the enduring allure of the rue Campagne-Première. A number of leading *Montparnos*, as members of the Montparnasse art colony were known, had flats or studios on that legendary Left Bank street, among them photographers Eugène Atget and Man Ray and painters Amedeo Modigliani, Nicholas de Staël, and Yves Klein. During the 1990s, it was the movie and recording stars who practically lived in its resident bistro, as much as its apartments, that helped keep the rue Campagne-Première in vogue. When the charismatic namesake owner hand-picked Alain Cirelli to buy her bistro, the new chef/owner was one of many who correctly assumed most of the celebrities would follow her out the door. A good guy, as Natacha described him, but hardly a compelling personality, Cirelli sought attention just as Natacha had planned it: through his cooking. "I want someone who does it in the kitchen," she reportedly told him. "You better buy it fast." He gained notice early and often by avoiding trendy and tricky ideas in favor of what he calls *cuisine française conviviale*. Although the odd Italian word—*mascarpone, carpaccio*—slips into menu descriptions, Cirelli wins plaudits in newspapers and fashion magazines for the likes of *hachis parmentier* (page 105), a peasant dish no more glamorous than its English equivalent, shepherd's pie. A proponent of long cooking, which is akin to slow food but has no organized movement, he prepares sweetbreads, veal knuckles, beef cheeks, and other hard-core bistro meats with simplicity and finesse. The updated tastes of the rue Campagne-Première are displayed on a bookshelf in the dining room. A Picasso monograph sits beside *Larousse Gastronomique.* Coffee-table books featuring the colorful creations of French chef Joël Robuchon and Russian painter Wassily Kandinsky stand back to back.

L'OURCINE

92, rue Broca; 13th
01 47 07 18 48
Métro: Les Gobelins
(pages 55, 148, 160)

If one could fairly assess a restaurant by its chef's résumé, as French food critics too often do, then L'Ourcine might have been the bistro of a Parisian diner's wildest dreams, combining the regionally riveted rigor of La Régalade's former chef Yves Camdeborde with the sweet-savory divergences of L'Épi Dupin's François Pasteau. But though Sylvain Danière esteems his prior employers as mentors, his menu at L'Ourcine positions him firmly in the Camdeborde camp. Danière finds innovation not in unconventional spicing, his chile-spiced quince marmalade notwithstanding, but rather in giving new life to overlooked or underrated foods, introducing, for example, the luxury that is foie gras to lowly but delicious pork cheeks. Danière is a chef with soft hands who brings an elegance and,

at times, a daintiness to lusty country cooking. As such, the bistro's tasteful but spare decor, with little ornamentation about the burgundy wainscoting, is nearly as good an indication of Danière's cooking style as his CV.

LA RÉGALADE

49, avenue Jean Moulin; 14th
01 45 45 68 58
Métro: Alésia
(pages 65, 98, 134, 150)

The French colloquialism *maso* (pronounced "mah-zo" and short for *masochiste*), though a harsh catchall for self-destructiveness, was insufficient to characterize the bold career move made by Bruno Doucet in the spring of 2004. When this young chef with a résumé as astutely assembled as any mille-feuille pastry purchased La Régalade, the most acclaimed bistro in Paris, from Yves Camdeborde, the spiritual father of Parisian gastro-bistro cuisine and already something of a Parisian culinary legend at the age of thirty-nine, Doucet's colleagues were describing the move as *kamikaze*. Not out to fulfill a death wish, Doucet wisely kept most of the bistro's decor and dining-room staff and instituted changes to the menu at a glacial pace. When my good friend and reliable bistro informant David Brower observed that Camdeborde's cherished black risotto was looking greener than before (a little more parsley?), Doucet seemed impressed and also a little alarmed. He was untroubled, however, by the regulars who refused to give him so much as a chance. To the disappointment of many, if not Doucet himself, the deserters were ultimately too few in number to ease the reservations backlog. In the end, Camdeborde's successor was just too good a chef and too easy a target to merit disapproval.

LE REPAIRE DE CARTOUCHE

99, rue Amelot; 11th
01 47 00 25 86
Métro: St-Sébastien-Froissart
(pages 54, 102, 153)

To avert any misunderstanding, I used to warn friends to meet me at Le Repaire de Cartouche on the rue Amelot and not the one on the boulevard des Filles-du-Calvaire, as others first cautioned me. I continue to do so as much out of habit as out of mischief, long after having discovered the two locations share the same menu, chef, kitchen, and connecting stairway. Seen from either entrance on parallel streets, the bistro's hundred-year-old faux-auberge decor always seems to impress French diners more than it does foreign ones. They are comforted by the very trappings we tend to dismiss as trite. There is little disagreement, however, about chef-owner Rodolphe Paquin's ability to make something new and exciting out of something old. Although much of Paquin's food and instincts are from his native Normandy, the creative push comes from Paris and a small band of bistro chefs bringing exacting standards and techniques to peasant cooking. Paquin stands out from a group that includes chefs Thierry Breton, Thierry Faucher, Stéphane Jégo, and ringleader Yves Camdeborde, first because he is the tallest among them but also for his special knack for finding affordable and unsung wines, many from the Languedoc region.

BRASSERIES

BALZAR

49, rue des Écoles; 5th
01 43 54 13 67
Métro: Cluny La Sorbonne
(pages 84, 136, 156)

In his book *Paris to the Moon*, published in 2000, Adam Gopnik repeated an assertion he had made two years earlier in a *New Yorker* article. The Balzar, the magazine's Paris correspondent wrote, "happens to be the best restaurant in the world." His was bold and fabulously absurb praise for a noteworthy brasserie that had never pursued or achieved greatness in any widely accepted measure that would put it in a class with Taillevent, or for that matter, Arthur Bryant's Kansas City barbecue. Furthermore, intermittently mediocre food would figure to be a disqualifying characteristic. But if "the best restaurant" is taken to mean the one whose alteration, relocation, or closing you would grieve most, then there was an argument to be made for Balzar, especially in 1998. At that time, the canteen of Sorbonne professors and Latin Quarter editors and intellectuals was about to be swallowed up by the Flo Restaurant Group. More intimate and, as a late-twentieth-century literary haunt, more relevant than its Montparnasse contemporaries, the bookish Balzar's individuality was particularly vulnerable to corporate takeover and standardization. As soon as one personality is interchangeable with another, be it that of a chef, a waiter, or an habitué, the special theater of the place is lost and, with it, the imperative of a good seat. I'm convinced the Flo Group understood what was special about Balzar and did not ruin it. With the jolly Christian René, formerly a Michelin-starred chef, running the kitchen, old standards like onion soup gratinée, roast leg of lamb, and baba au rhum (page 156) are as good as before, while the overall quality has if anything improved from the time immediately before the transition. I wouldn't know where to find a better version of classic poached skate wing in brown butter sauce and, thanks to René, have very little incentive to go looking for one. Six years into Balzar's Flo era, French scholar Gilles Kepel could have been speaking for many when, reminded of the widely lamented change in ownership over a plate of *steak frites*, he noted with an apologetic shrug that there was nowhere else to go. In Paris of all places, those are no small words.

BOFINGER

5, rue de la Bastille; 4th
01 42 72 87 82
Métro: Bastille
(pages 38, 86)

Since only 74 of Bofinger's 270 seats are situated beneath the stained-glass cupola that transforms its main dining room into a resplendent cathedral of the Belle Époque, its floor managers have difficulty filling the endless requests for tables under the *verrière*. Those led up the copper-railed staircase should not, however, feel as though they're destined for a Siberia, although Siberia is a very small corner of the decoration. The five continents are depicted in the exquisite period marquetry that adorns the more intimate, upper-lever dining parlors. The division between choice tables and less desirable ones is more a question of time than geography. Families, businesspeople, and tourists generally prefer to dine early. A more glamorous and theatrical crowd sups late, 9 at the earliest and more often 10, 10:30, or whenever the Opéra Bastille lets out. Choucroute is this official historic monument's landmark dish. The only issue in doubt is which choucroute, the classic with smoked pork and sausages or its fish counterpart. Early or late, the multitiered oyster platters work on all levels.

BRASSERIE LIPP

151, boulevard Saint-Germain; 6th
01 45 48 53 91
Métro: St-Germain-des-Prés
(page 122)

The sale of Lipp to the Bertrand Group, completed in 2002, did little to change the interior topography maintained by the Cazes family during the eighty-two years they owned this great Parisian classic and choreographed its celebrated comings and goings. Most changes have been subtle ones quietly lamented by veteran staffers and habitués. The one noticeable difference is that the hosts no longer argue with diners who regard being led to the upstairs dining room—Lipp's Siberia—as an insult. Seldom do they resort to the tired tale of Madonna having thrown a party up there. "It's a disadvantage for us," concedes current general manager Claude Guittard. "No one wants to climb those stairs." Though reservations are honored and requests for main-level tables are entertained,

there is nothing egalitarian about seating assignments. First priority goes to regulars, who are treated like members of a club. Without booking they are nevertheless assured of a table and instant access to the leeks vinaigrette, sole meunière, or *cervelas rémoulade* (garlicky pork sausage with piquant mayonnaise) they've been eating for thirty years, even if making room for them means reducing the average amount of space between tables from four inches to three. Next come A-list celebrities from the political, literary, and showbiz worlds, many of whom wind up with a place along *le rang de radiateur*, "radiator row," the sixteen well-heated places along or facing the banquette on the right side of the main dining room. If you're seated here it either means you're important or you've arrived two hours before everyone else. The occupancy of the *centre-gauche*, or center-left (named for its location, not political orientation), is determined less by snobbery than the tastes of the headwaiters, who amuse themselves with a silly nightly contest: Who can fill that section with the most beautiful women?

LA COUPOLE

102, boulevard du Montparnasse; 14th
01 43 20 14 20
Métro: Vavin
(pages 44, 114, 141, 183)

Opened in 1927 to lure away the hordes of artists, writers, loafers, lost souls, and revelers then congregating at other brasseries and cafés on the boulevard Montparnasse, La Coupole's jazzy mosaic floors, Art Deco lighting, thirty-seven muraled pillars, and ten-thousand-square-foot expanse marked the cupola-crowned summit of a great Parisian idea: the brasserie as grand and glamorous, all-inclusive café-bar-restaurant ballroom rendezvous. It is a relic that, for all its magnificence, is sometimes compared unfavorably to its romanticized former self. Béatrice, the woman who answers the reservations line, can put your name down for a good table, perhaps the corner tables—83, 130, 141, or 152—prized by couples, but she can't seat you next to Pablo Picasso or James Joyce. It's nothing personal. The kitchen and dining-room staffs at La Coupole are unburdened by the brasserie's past. They've enough to do seating diners, taking orders, preparing and serving food, turning tables, and loading seafood platters in a frenetic beehive while not crashing into colleagues smoothly scurrying to do the same. I do wish Paul Delbard, a very capable chef and manager, could pare down the menu to the things his kitchen already does well and could be doing with greater consistency, among them fish soup, grilled *andouillette* (sausage of pork intestines), and La Coupole's famous lamb curry (page 114). But then La Coupole would be getting away from the inclusive, something-for-everyone-at-any-hour spirit of a true brasserie.

GALLOPIN

40, rue Notre-Dame-des-Victoires; 2nd
01 42 36 45 38
Métro: Bourse
(page 184)

❀ ❀ ❀ ❀ ❀ ❀ ❀ ❀ ❀ ❀ ❀ ❀ ❀ ❀ ❀ ❀ ❀ ❀

In the late 1870s, wine and beer merchant Gustave Gallopin expanded his retail bar opposite the Corinthian columns of the Bourse (the Paris stock exchange) and opened the city's first *bar américain*, as brasseries modeled after American cocktail bars and lounges were first known. Decorated in

high Victorian style, with Cuban mahogany walls, bar, and furniture crafted by London artisans and spectacular glass, copper, and mosaic decoration, Gallopin would soon serve as the unofficial headquarters of bankers and brokers, who dispatched their buy, sell, and hold orders from within. Oddly, this distinguished dispenser of cocktails and, for celebrations of fortunes made, Champagne (by the mid-twentieth century only cabarets sold more of it) is most famous for its silver tankards just short of a half-pint. In the universe of ales, a twenty-centiliter mug, as opposed to the twenty-five-centiliter standard, is called a Gallopin of beer. Following decades of fading fortunes, especially in the financial sector, Gallopin the brasserie was meticulously restored by Marie-Louise and Georges Alexandre, former proprietors of Bofinger. The ex-owners of Paris's first brasserie had purchased the city's first *bar américain*. At night they now cater to a theatrical crowd, meaning diners who either work in the theater, attend the theater, or like to see some theater when they dine. Order steak tartare or crêpes Alexandre (page 184), the house rendition of crêpes Suzette, and you are treated to silver tableside service of the highest style and greatest flourish.

LE GRAND COLBERT

2, rue Vivienne; 2nd
01 42 86 87 88
Métro: Bourse
(pages 116, 128, 151)

❀ ❀ ❀ ❀ ❀ ❀ ❀ ❀ ❀ ❀ ❀ ❀ ❀ ❀ ❀ ❀ ❀ ❀

When writer-director Nancy Meyers chose this historic monument as the setting for the penultimate scene in her film *Something's Gotta Give*, starring Diane Keaton, Jack Nicholson, and Keanu Reeves, she was ignoring one simple fact. Though the script called for Keaton to laud the brasserie for serving the best roast chicken in the universe, Le Grand Colbert did not serve roast chicken, good or bad, and by all indications had not from the time the 1830 space between the rue Vivienne and the galerie Colbert became a brasserie. During the months leading up to the film's 2003 release, chef William Laurent and his staff were working frantically to come up with a credible, best-in-the-universe roast chicken. They feared, correctly as it turned out, that once the film was out, many diners would stop ordering his sensational grilled lamb steaks with garlic butter sauce, gratin Dauphinois (potatoes baked in cream), and *tomates à la provençale* with fuming thyme incense (if only she'd praised the lamb steaks) and start demanding *poulet rôti*. Although his kitchen's renditions of various brasserie classics are hardly exceptional, Laurent does excel with presentations that require fanfare and, as the French say, *cinéma*. Desserts like baba au rhum, Mont Blanc (chestnut cream meringue), crème caramel, and the flambéed kitsch classic *omelette norvégienne* (baked Alaska) come to mind. This flair for the dramatic is shared by the brasserie's destination *maître d'hôtel*: Concierges from deluxe hotels will send their guests to Le Grand Colbert on the nights they know Laurent Berenguier will be there to greet, serve, tease, and otherwise charm them. Lured away from a rival brasserie, Berenguier's current office is a resplendent, twenty-foot-high dining room with etched glass partitions, tufted leather banquettes, hand-painted, polychromatic frescoes, and other flourishes of nineteenth-century decoration.

JULIEN

16, rue du Faubourg Saint-Denis; 10th
01 47 70 12 06
Métro: Strasbourg St-Denis
(pages 90, 180)

The drama of entering Julien, of instantly stepping into a radically different time, place, and social sphere, is surpassed only by the jolt of leaving Julien. Beholding this Belle Époque jewel amid the Turkish grills, garment wholesalers, and grimy building façades of the rue du Faubourg Saint-Denis is one of those wondrously unexpected surprises afforded the Parisian *flâneur*, or stroller, in the city's overlooked sections. But finding yourself deposited back on Faubourg Saint-Denis and its miasma of kebab grease and vehicular exhaust after having passed an enchanted hour or two enveloped in full Art Nouveau splendor is a shock to mind and body. Back inside, diners not yet finished with their Champagne and their chocolate-sauced profiteroles—and where better to have them?—appear to be wrapped in the vines of the floral and vegetal ornamentation that decorates the circa 1902 walls and ceiling. Many have already forgiven Julien's formulaic menu. The actors, designers, and bourgeois bohemians who either inhabit or work in the Strasbourg–Saint-Denis area of the 10th arrondissement are fast becoming permanent fixtures, just like the beautiful women of Alphonse Mucha's "The Four Seasons" depicted here in the spectacular period murals of Louis Trézel. If only the first step out the door were not so brutal.

AU PIED DE COCHON

6, rue Coquillière; 1st
01 40 13 77 00
Metro: Châtelet Les Halles/Louvre Rivoli
(pages 66, 74)

Open 24/7, Au Pied de Cochon takes the brasserie precept of continuous service to the limit. When the seven-story Les Halles institution was completely remodeled in 1985, the construction was completed from the top floor down, reversing the usual order, to keep at least part of the brasserie open for the longest period possible. A nocturnal Paris fueled by onion soup, oysters on the half shell, Beaujolais wines, and *pied de cochon grillé, sauce béarnaise*—grilled pig's foot with béarnaise saucé—endured without this municipal utility for a mere six weeks, when work on the ground floor denied access to all levels. No longer a wee-hours haunt for the poultry butchers and fishmongers of Les Halles, whose wholesale food markets left town in 1970, Au Pied de Cochon reopened as a more polished brasserie *du luxe* catering to revelers, businesspeople, the pre- and post-theater crowd, tourists, families, and lovers with nothing to hide. A veteran dining-room brigade led by Jean-François Lecerf, who arrived here in 1964, maintains a continuity to the past somewhat lacking in the splashy decor. You won't spot more than a couple of those dependable men in black, though, working the overnight shift, which is akin to duty in a fire station. Most of the time it is very quiet. But every now and then a pack of nightclubbers stumbles in, the alarm bells go off in the kitchen, and, depending on the condition of the group as much as the hour of the morning, either the Champagne or the black coffee cannot be poured quickly enough.

BRASSERIE WEPLER

14, place de Clichy; 18th
01 45 22 53 24
Métro: Place de Clichy
(pages 60, 62, 89, 174)

Among the last of the classic Parisian brasseries to remain independent, the Wepler probably lacks the requisite *chichi* and *fioritures*, "flourishes," to be a tempting takeover target of large restaurant groups. For an establishment that opened in 1892 and came of age in the 1920s there is precious little Art Nouveau or Art Deco decoration and no great art. Among the past habitués spilling down to the place de Clichy from Montmartre and Pigalle, Picasso, Utrillo, and Modigliani chose not to settle their bills with canvases that might have taken the place of the kitschy wall murals. The grooming and tailoring displayed by the headwaiters in this new century, as in the last, are often comically amiss, as if to parody the perfectionism demanded of their counterparts at La Coupole or Bofinger. Yet due in no small measure to these shortcomings, the Wepler maintains a special authenticity. It does not feel touristy, though foreign accents are everywhere. It does not feel like a literary landmark, though there are writers, actors, musicians, artists, or at least con artists seated at every other table. And the food does not feel like it's out of a factory, though it is hastily dispatched by an assembly line of cooks and, for the seafood platters that make up a third of Wepler's business, a hurried crew of oyster shuckers. The choucroute with salmon and slab bacon is the great brasserie choucroute you never hear or read much about, which, like the Wepler itself, is a big part of its appeal.

WINE BARS

LE BARATIN

8, rue Jouye-Rouve; 20th
01 43 49 39 70
Métro: Pyrénées
(pages 52, 112, 164)

* *

The word *fusion* somehow does not fit the multi-cultural cooking of Raquel Carena, the Italian Argentine who, with Philippe Pinoteau, owns this beloved neighborhood wine bar with a far-reaching reputation. Though her *plats du jour* assume various South American, Mediterranean, Asian, and French accents, the results never seem contrived. Only she can lace as traditional a French dish as veal blanquette with ginger, lemon-grass, curry powder, and cinnamon without the effort appearing trendy or manufactured. That each preparation can be confused for authentic home cooking, no matter its mixed origins and inventions, attests to Carena's instinctive feel for flavors and ingredients. She's an adaptive cook. It also helps that the Bellevue locale, with its weathered woodwork, broken tile mosaic, and crammed seating under a regional wine map of France and a vintage photograph of a bistro storefront by some-time habitué Willy Ronis, looks so genuine and so much older than anything born in 1988. Carena's partner has a natural feel for wines and the conversations around them, not really unexpected from a guy named Pinoteau. Both participant in and arbiter of the small discussion groups that form nightly around his bar, Pinoteau effectively shapes the *baratin*, French for "chatter," in Le Baratin.

LA CAVE À L'OS À MOELLE

181, rue Lourmel; 15th
01 45 57 28 28
Métro: Lourmel
(pages 29, 30, 64, 72, 81, 168)

* *

Directly across the street from the kitchen of his superb bistro, L'Os à Moelle, chef-owner Thierry Faucher has reinvented the concept of a *bar à vin*. A few yards back of the zinc-style counter that fronts his wine bar annex, diners must get up now and then from their shared communal country tables to feed themselves. Farmhouse lunches and dinners are served *table d'hôte* (buffet style), begin-

ning with cold appetizers, terrines, and steamed *bulots* and *bigorneauxs* (two kinds of sea snails), continuing with soups and stews kept warm over an antique stove, and concluding with cheeses and desserts. It's *cuisine de grand-mère*, only the grandmother is a great bistro chef in *his* late thirties who's cooked in some of the best restaurant kitchens in Paris. Wines are browsed and chosen by hand from wall displays as you would books from library shelves. Distressed brick walls provide a rustic backdrop for scratched plates, worn cloth napkins, and third-generation cookware. Still, what impressed me more than the flea-market chic was a quiet gesture of small-town kindness from a server to an old man who couldn't grasp the *table d'hôte* concept. He had wandered in for lunch only because he assumed any place with *l'os à moelle* (marrowbone) in its name had to specialize in that delicacy. Although the wine bar ordinarily does not serve marrowbone, the server nodded, jogged out the door and across the rue Lourmel, tapped on Faucher's kitchen window, and placed a take-out order.

L'Estaminet d'Aromes et Cépages

41, rue de Bretagne; 3rd
01 43 72 18 77
Métro: Filles de Calvaire
(page 170)

To name the adorable wine bar he opened in the Marais quarter in 2002, Thierry Poncin chose the word *estaminet*, a synonym for *bistro* that's been out of use for nearly as long as the two-room printer's workshop in which it is housed. Poncin's *estaminet* is an immediate extension, physically as well as philosophically, of Aromes et Cépages, his

wine stall in the Marché des Enfants Rouges. Food shoppers and merchants at the oldest covered market in Paris (it was founded in 1615) can purchase one of the organic wines displayed in the retail shop, transport it some twenty feet to the wine bar, and, for a 5-euro (about $7) corkage fee, very carefully assess its merits. Considerate of his clients' needs, Poncin serves an unflimsy and unfussy *plat du jour* at lunchtime and tapas-style small plates composed of the highest quality cured meats and fish throughout the afternoon. Out front, the secluded terrace, unseen from the busy rue de Bretagne, is a magical spot some but thankfully not too many people consider for a late-in-the-day aperitif.

Juvéniles

47, rue de Richelieu; 1st
01 42 97 46 49
Métro: Palais Royal Musée du Louvre, Bourse
(page 26)

Having split with Mark Williamson, his partner here and at Willi's Wine Bar, Scottish expat Tim Johnston is freer than ever to express his likes and dislikes and chide his fellow Parisian merchants, usually without consequence. "I'm a bit on the outside," he says, somewhat understandable when you serve Scottish haggis—minced sheep's organs and oatmeal stuffed into sheep's stomach lining—at your Parisian wine bar. "They don't regard me as competition." Among the French capital's first and greatest champions of southern Rhône wines, Johnston is so enamored of Syrah, among that region's resident red wine varietals, that he describes the grape as "the meaning of life." Lately he's emerged as a passionate advocate of screw caps. "I have put up with corked bottles for too long," he says, defiantly unscrewing a bottle of Fronsac. Many such bottles sit in the unpacked cases that have filled this slapdash little wine bar since its 1985 opening. Johnston compiles his roster of wines by the glass as he would a soccer team, filling its eleven positions with three French reds, three imported reds, a serious white in the crucial center fullback position, a couple of thirst-quenching whites as role players, a Champagne, and a new discovery. Beyond good charcuterie and English cheeses, Juvéniles' Sri Lankan cooks do a pretty good job with tapas-like dishes and various bistro whims.

LE ROUGE-GORGE

8, rue Saint-Paul; 4th
01 48 04 75 89
Métro: Sully Morland, St-Paul
(pages 28, 40)

A hydrolic engineer in an earlier life, François Briclot is a great backer of Corsican wines not only at his Le Marais wine bar but in bistros, restaurants, and wine bars throughout Paris. Still, it can't be the Corsican wines, no matter their charms, that draw enough stylish women into his corner establishment to often outnumber their male counterparts, well groomed or not. If Le Rouge-Gorge manages at times to resemble a tea salon more than it does a *bar à vin*, traditionally a masculine domain, it has more to do with Briclot's catering to the artsy yet urbane Parisians who inhabit this historic and now high-rent neighborhood. Occupying the ground and cellar levels of a seventeenth-century house, Le Rouge-Gorge is, at a glance, casual and rustic. Yet much thought and

know-how went into its look, from the marble-topped bar and copper sink to the old placards hung on the stone walls. The wine list is the wine cellar. All are encouraged to descend to the old *cave* and choose a bottle themselves from a collection of what Briclot calls *vins d'auteur*, by which he means boutique wines that reflect the personality of the impassioned growers who produce them. He describes one such winemaker, Jean-François Meriau, as "elegant in his rusticity." He might have been talking about himself or, with a change of the pronoun, his wine bar. His regulars might wish he were talking about them.

LE VERRE VOLÉ

67, rue Lancry; 10th
01 48 03 17 34
Métro: Jacques Bonsergent
(page 49)

Among the innovations pioneered by Cyril Bordarier at Le Verre Volé was a new interior design style he called *bordelique*—French for "messy." It entailed his filling every inch of a small storefront near the Canal Saint-Martin with a scattered assortment of chairs, tables, crates, utensils, and things; lining its walls with wine bottles posed upright on narrow shelves; wedging a barely serviceable kitchenette with not much more than a foot of counter space into the rear left corner; and, in 2000, quickly launching his novel wine bar/boutique. At the time of its opening, the now trendy district was still in the early stages of its dramatic revitalization. Le Verre Volé's disorder fit the local vibe and turned the wine bar into a nightly block party. It helped too that Bordarier was fulfilling a timeless ethos of Parisian living: You can be very happy without many of the comforts others take for granted as long as you have a good cheese, fresh bread, and a decent bottle of wine. At Le Verre Volé that decent bottle costs only 5 euros (about $6.50) above retail and could be chosen from a continually expanding selection of the so-called *vins naturels*, meaning organic wines produced without fining agents (primarily used to clarify wines), filtration, or added sulfites. Lacking the infrastructure and equipment to do any real cooking, Bordarier has always compensated by procuring first-rate products, be it the artisanal Brittany butter of Jean-Yves Bordier, the hams from Joël Meurdesoif's acclaimed Left Bank charcuterie, or the canned sardines of La Compagnie Bretonne du Poisson. Those sardines are served in their cans: Bordarier is either too proud of their noble origin to remove them from their tin or just too *bordelique* to bother.

LA MUSE VIN

101, rue de Charonne; 11th
01 40 09 93 05
Métro: Charonne
(pages 61, 92)

The floor-to-ceiling displays of standing wine bottles resemble those at Le Verre Volé. The selling of those wines for only 5 euros (about $6.50) above their retail price, the gentlest of corkage fees, is the same as the policy Le Verre Volé initiated several years earlier. Indeed, La Muse Vin is a terrific tribute to and enhancement of a great new wine bar format, even if none of the principals involved see it exactly that way. Co-owners Olivier Dubois and Olivier Dupré aren't merely wine experts. The *deux* Oliviers are passionate fans who treat wine appreciation like a spectator sport. If you catch them

mid-discussion it can sound like they're rating soccer prospects ("...has some muscle and kick... only gets better in three to five years...where's the finish?"). Their infectious enthusiasm is not without snobbery, but it seems to come more from the heart than the turned-up nose. Their idea of a find is not merely a wine from a small producer in an unsung or emerging region but one that features a grape with which that area is not ordinarily associated, for example, a Chardonnay from the Loire Valley, traditionally the province of Sauvignon Blanc and Chenin Blanc. The contemporary and deceptively simply bistro cooking is thoughtfully prepared and plated with outstanding ingredients and, whenever possible, an emphasis on the salty, smoky, and spicy flavors that pose the greatest challenges to matchmakers of food and wine.

LA PETITE SYRAH

15, rue Joseph de Maistre, 18th
01 42 54 35 46
Métro: Blanche, Abbesses
(page 144)

The *petite* in the title fits the dimensions of this deceptively plain *bar à vin*, but not the size and ambitions of its wine list. If wine dealer Alain Beunon, the proprietor, wanted to widen his selection he'd have to learn to write much smaller first. The blackboards that cover the walls are completely filled with the scripted wine list. There is barely enough space for the hyphen between *Crozes* and *Hermitage*, among the featured Rhône Valley reds made from the Syrah grape. More impressive than the number of bottles is the variety of similitude: You'll often find three or four examples of a little-known wine, when at other wine bars you'd be lucky to find one. Beunon wants us to flit from bottle to bottle. Two things can be said about the food program consisting of charcuterie plates and a couple of bistro-styled *plats du jour*. It's continually changing shape and it's always pretty good. La Petite Syrah, though situated close to the heart of Montmartre, is largely ignored by the hordes piling into the flashy bars, scenic cafés, and assorted tourist traps nearby. Maybe that's all the better for a wine flitter's paradise, where obscurity is so often a source of discovery and fascination.

WILLI'S WINE BAR

13, rue des Petits Champs; 1st
01 42 61 05 09
Métro: Palais Royal Musée du Louvre
(pages 22, 25, 85)

* * * * * * * * * * * * * * * * * * *

The impact of Willi's innovations are all the more extraordinary for just how commonplace they've become. Before Willi's, Parisian wine bars generally did feature wines from numerous unsung regions in and outside of France with the names of their producers. Few were changing their wine lists on a regular basis. While most wine bars were proffering familiarity with their selections, Mark "Willi" Williamson's was proposing discovery. And no other true wine bar was taking its food preparations and food and wine pairings so seriously. Willi's democratization of the *bar à vin* hasn't completely shut out wine snobbery, but it has kept its rotated pleasures accessible and affordable for diners, sippers, and gulpers alike. French wines by the glass sell for as little as 3.50 euros (about $4.50 and pretty low for this high-rent district). "France has a talent for producing great wines for very little money," says Williamson, an influential champion of wines from the Rhône Valley, the Loire Valley, Alsace, Cahors, Madiran, and Provence. "You can drink wonderful little Côtes de Provence endlessly without getting a call from your bank manager the next morning."

INDEX